SWITCHED ON
Science

Second Edition

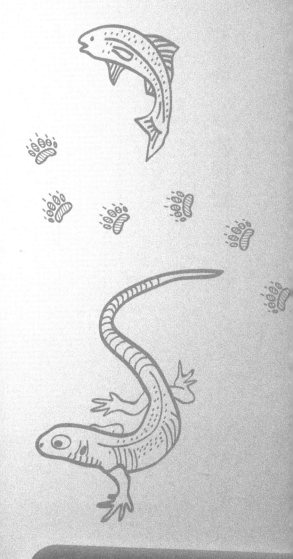

Teacher's Guide

Essential digital resources available on

MY RISING STARS

www.risingstars-uk.com

GW00790164

Although every effort has been made to ensure that website addresses are correct at time of going to press, Rising Stars cannot be held responsible for the content of any website mentioned in this book. It is sometimes possible to find a relocated web page by typing in the address of the home page for a website in the URL window of your browser.

Hachette UK's policy is to use papers that are natural, renewable and recyclable products and made from wood grown in sustainable forests. The logging and manufacturing processes are expected to conform to the environmental regulations of the country of origin.

Orders: please contact Bookpoint Ltd, 130 Park Drive, Milton Park, Abingdon, Oxon OX14 4SE. Telephone: (44) 01235 400555. Email: primary@bookpoint.co.uk.

Lines are open from 9 a.m. to 5 p.m., Monday to Saturday, with a 24-hour message answering service. Visit our website at www.risingstars-uk.com for details of the full range of Rising Stars publications.

Online support and queries email: onlinesupport@risingstars-uk.com

ISBN: 978 1 51043607 7

© Rising Stars UK Ltd 2018

First published in 2018 by
Rising Stars UK Ltd, part of the Hodder Education Group
An Hachette UK Company
Carmelite House
50 Victoria Embankment
London EC4Y 0DZ

www.risingstars-uk.com

Impression number 1
Year   2018

Author: Rosemary Feasey

Publisher: Laura White

Logo design: Burville-Riley Partnership

Typesetting: Aptara

Cover design: Marc Burville-Riley

Artwork: Steph Dix (GCI for Illustration) and Aptara

Printed by Ashford Colour Press

A catalogue record for this title is available from the British Library.

Contents

How to use Switched on Science, Second Edition

HOW THE YEAR 1 TOPICS FIT WITH THE NATIONAL CURRICULUM

In England, the primary science curriculum has been written to indicate the basic entitlement for children at Key Stage 1. *Switched on Science, Second Edition,* Year 1 ensures full coverage of the content for this year group with learning objectives at the beginning of each activity indicating the curriculum link. Children are given access to the Key Stage 1 curriculum in different contexts providing appropriate repetition and reinforcement. Units also provide contexts for learning in areas they experienced in EYFS and will meet in Key Stage 2 and are highlighted for the teacher.

What is included in the printed and online resources?

At the beginning of each topic learning outcomes for working scientifically are listed as well as subject knowledge concept statements.

The introduction for each topic also lists pupil videos which can be used to introduce new concepts and consolidate learning, and CPD videos which can be used to build confidence in teaching science. These can be accessed via the *My Rising Stars* website. Also online are editable versions of the Activity resources, teaching PowerPoints, interactive activities and visual resources to engage your pupils, as well as PDF versions of the Teacher's Guide.

Cross-curricular topic webs

We have taken a topic approach, which fits well with how most schools teach Key Stage1 science. Each year is organised into six topics, providing half a term's work. There is also a photocopiable section at the end of Year 1 and 2 Teacher's Guides that provides activities for developing the Seasonal change aspect of the curriculum over two years. The material is extensive and presents additional opportunities for children to develop and consolidate their understanding of plants, animals and the weather over the school year.

Topics have been organised in such a way that schools can either follow the suggested route or rearrange the topics to suit themselves.

At the beginning of each topic is a cross-curricular planning overview to indicate the potential of the topic across different curriculum areas.

Role play

For some topics there are suggestions for science role-play to encourage additional exploration.

Get started

There is an initial starter activity for all topics, which aims to elicit what children already know via interesting starting points.

Scientific vocabulary

As an important element of the science curriculum, and of course literacy, each topic has a list of words with which children should become familiar through listening, reading and writing on a regular basis.

To support children's understanding of key vocabulary and challenging ideas, some words have been defined so that they are more accessible.

Useful websites

You will find a list of useful websites with free resources or an interesting video that links to the topic on *My Rising Stars*. Put them in your favourites so that you can access them whenever needed.

Health and safety

Issues relating to health and safety are highlighted at the beginning of each topic and teachers are always advised to refer to their copy of:
ASE Be Safe! 4th Edition (9780863574269) available from www.ase.org.uk.

Reference is also made to **CLEAPSS** science, cleapss.org.uk, which also provides safety advice and suggestions for activities for primary schools.

You will need

Each activity includes a list of the key equipment and resources that are required to carry out the activities in each topic.

Assessment

Key Stage 1 material is written in such a way that opportunities for teacher assessment are an integral part of the activities.

At the beginning of each activity, learning objectives (L.O.) are listed and, at the end of each activity, there are suggested assessments for:

o Emerging (Em.)

o Expected (Exp.)

o Exceeded (Exc.)

In addition, there are interactive activities that can be used to assess children's understanding of each topic. These can be found on the *My Rising Stars* website.

Activity resources

The Activity resources section contains photocopiable resources for children to use. You will find diagrams for labelling, flashcards, tables, posters and instruction sheets.

Access to online resources

All teachers in your school can get access to the digital resources, which include CPD videos, pupil videos, editable resource sheets, word mats, interactive activities, planning and overview word docs on the *My Rising Stars* website. To get access, each teacher can simply register or login at www.risingstars-uk.com.

SEASONAL CHANGE

The Seasonal change section at the end of the book is an important element of the curriculum; its aim is to develop children's understanding of how their environment changes across the year, and how humans also change in what they wear, eat and do. It is appropriate that children develop their understanding of this across Key Stage 1 for the following reasons:

o Seasonal change repeats, children should have experience of comparing what happened when they were in Year 1 with Year 2. What were the similarities and differences? What is repeated?

o Placing learning about plants and animals in just one term means that children only learn about the living things in their environment during that time.

o Studying habitats regularly throughout the year allows children to observe and record change.

o Studying habitats regularly throughout the year means that they will learn about plants and animals that appear at different times of the year.

o Visiting the local environment across the year means that children get a 'second bite' at learning, e.g. observation, identifying and naming plants and animals so that by the end of Key Stage 1 children are confident and competent in naming living things.

o Recording observations of Seasonal change allows children to look back and compare similarities and differences between the season.

o Year 2 children can progress in deepening and broadening their understanding of local habitats and begin to use standard measurements in observations, e.g. temperature.

Many schools are adopting an approach where Seasonal change is developed over a year with teachers timetabling regular visits into the school grounds or local park, e.g. fortnightly for an hour. During each visit, the children carry out a range of activities including 'Adopt a tree' or habitat and record changes, e.g. photograph each visit.

Some teachers use a 'Big Book' approach where children record their observations of Seasonal change over a year in Year 1, and then the Big Book goes with the class to Year 2 so that they can look back and continue their work in Year 2.

For Year 1, the Seasonal change unit is divided into six sections, each covering a two-month period. Year 2 is the same but it builds on and extends learning from Year 1.

TOPIC 1 Who am I?

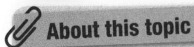

About this topic

Curriculum link: Year 1, Animals, including humans

SUMMARY:

In this topic, children will learn about the basic parts of the human body and explore their five senses using a wide range of activities, which can be spread over a half term and from which the teacher can choose where appropriate.

UNITS:

1.1: My body 1.2: My senses

ACTIVITY RESOURCES:

- 1.1: How do I feel?   • 1.2: Eye chart

- 1.3: Appointment booking form
- 1.4: Parts of my body cards
- 1.5: Taste me cards

ONLINE RESOURCES:

Teaching slides (Powerpoint): Who am I?

Interactive activity: Who am I?

CPD video: Who am I?

Pupil video: Who am I?

Word mat: Who am I?

Editable Planning: Who am I?

Topic Test: Who am I?

Learning objectives

This topic covers the following learning objectives:

○ Identify, name, draw and label the basic parts of the human body.

○ Say which part of the body is associated with each sense.

Working scientifically skills

This topic develops the following working scientifically skills:

○ Observe closely, using simple equipment.

○ Identify and classify.

○ Gather and record data to help in answering questions.

CROSS-CURRICULAR LINKS

This topic offers the following cross-curricular opportunities:

Numeracy and mathematics

○ Read and write numbers when collecting data, e.g. eye colour, and represent as a pictogram.

○ Measure arm length and height. Record results using tables.

○ Sequence events in chronological order using time language, e.g. 'Before I was one, I could only crawl, after I was two, I went to nursery', etc.

English

○ Use key science vocabulary when talking and writing.

○ Draft and redraft sentences about what is done in science activities and use punctuation in sentences.

○ Read and follow instructions. Make and read body part labels.

○ Predict what will happen next.

○ Record sentences using microphones, Talk Cards or Talk Buttons and books.

○ Create a 'Who am I? Big Book' with an index and glossary.

○ Listen and re-tell the *Funnybones* story by Janet and Allan Ahlberg.

Geography

○ Find out where self, parents, grandparents and other family members were born.

○ Look up places using a map / atlas.

○ Give directions to someone who is blindfolded.

Computing / ICT

○ Input data to create a pictogram about eye colour, favourite foods, etc.

○ Use a computer to find out information about the body.

○ Use digital cameras to take photographs of objects around the school.

○ Use a digital microscope to look at hair, skin, fabrics.

Music

○ Learn and sing songs related to the body, e.g. 'Dem Bones', 'Heads, Shoulders, Knees and Toes'.

○ Use different parts of the body to make sounds.

History

- Create a personal timeline from birth to present and place significant events on the timeline, e.g. *moved house, started school, brother or sister born*.
- Find out about what parents and grandparents did, wore, or ate when they were the same age as the children.
- Ask children to find out what was an important event in the year that they were born.

Art

- Use different materials to create a sensory picture.
- Create a self-portrait using paints / Paint program.
- Create dough sculptures of themselves, in an action stance.

PE

- Create a dance sequence linked to music or use resource emotion cards (Activity Resource 1.1).
- Develop / improve a specific skill, e.g. throwing, catching, balancing.

HEALTH AND SAFETY

In this topic, some activities include food and tasting. Check for children with specific allergies also check for cultural norms each time there is a tasting /eating activity.

SUBJECT KNOWLEDGE

Sight

How the eye works is complex and, at this level, children need to know that in order to see objects we need light, so the opposite is true: without light (pure darkness) we cannot see things. At this stage, children may not have experienced complete darkness so think they can 'see' in the dark. Light is reflected off objects and travels in a straight line to the eye. The brain then makes sense of the signals sent from the eye to tell us what we can see.

Taste

Humans have taste buds (children can see these using a digital microscope). When we eat, the food rubs against the taste buds which send messages to the brain to tell us what the taste is. There are five tastes: sweet, sour, bitter, salty and umami (savoury, e.g. fish, mushrooms, yeast). Most children can recognise sweet, sour and salty, but may find bitter a difficult taste to identify. Sight and smell also play

STEAM (SCIENCE, TECHNOLOGY, ENGINEERING, ART AND MATHS) OPPORTUNITIES

Invite into class

- Nurse to talk to children about, for example, keeping healthy and their job.
- An optician and audiologist to talk about eyes and ears.
- Sports person or trainer to talk about keeping parts of the body fit and healthy.
- Storyteller or poet to encourage creative writing about themselves, using their senses, etc.

Visit

- Museums with interactive exhibits on the human body and the senses.
- An optician to see equipment and talk with staff.

an important part in taste. If we remove smell, the taste changes (try holding your nose as you eat a banana – what does it taste like?).

Touch

When we touch something, the nerves in our skin send messages to our brain which tells us whether something is hot or cold and what it feels like, such as sharp or sticky. We also sense pressure – something pushing against our skin.

Hearing

Sound is made when something moves or vibrates. Just as with light having a source, there are sources of sound. If you hit a drum, the part you hit (the skin) vibrates. This in turn vibrates (shakes) the air molecules next to the drum, which vibrates air molecules next to them until all the air molecules in your ear are vibrated. Inside the ear, tiny hairs then vibrate and messages are sent via nerves to the brain. As you move away from the source of the sound, it gets fainter because the sound has further to travel and as the vibration moves through the air, it doesn't only travel to your ear but in many other directions as well.

Smell

We smell something because it gives off particles that travel to our noses; tiny hairs inside it send signals to the brain that tell us what the smell is. Our brain tells us whether we like it or not.

SCIENTIFIC VOCABULARY: WHO AM I?

It is assumed that most Year 1 children know basic parts of the body, such as *eyes, ears, head, mouth* and *nose*, although they might not know how to write and spell them. You can download a Word mat of essential vocabulary for this topic from *My Rising Stars*.

backbone: the bones that run along the centre of the back; this is also called the spine

ear lobe: the fleshy part at the bottom of the ears

elbow: the joint between our upper arm and forearm; it is where we bend our arm

eye socket: part of the skull where the eye fits

hips: the hips help humans to support the weight of their body when they are standing or moving about; they help us to balance

joints: where bones meet, e.g. knee, elbow, shoulder, hips, ankle

ribs: the set of bones that curve from the spine round to the chest

thigh: the part of the leg that goes from the knee to the hip

tongue: in humans, the tongue is a muscle that is used for tasting, eating, swallowing and talking

vertebrae: the small bones that make up the backbone

nail: a thin, hard material covering the end of the fingers and toes in humans and some other animals

Key words: backbone / chin / ears / elbow / eye socket / eyes / fingers / foot / feet / head / hear / hearing / hip / human / joints / knee / leg / neck / nose / ribs / see / senses / sight / smell / spine / taste / thigh / toes / tongue / touch /vertebrae / wrist

 PREPARE THE CLASSROOM

Area 1: Photo gallery

o In this area, you could include photographs of children when they were younger and now; mix them up and challenge the children to identify and match the baby to the right member of the class. The same could be done with photographs of members of staff. Children explain how they know.

o A 'Big Book' photograph album where each child has a page for their own photographs, one for each year so far, with written comments of how they have changed.

o A 'Talking Photo Album' with a photograph of each child in the class. When children press the button, they can listen to the child's recorded message, e.g. what they are good at, what they like or a hobby.

 • Self-portraits by the children (these could be from an art session, or created using an IT package such as Paint) or children take photographs of each other using the emotions cards (Activity Resource 1.1). Children identify who has painted the portrait and explain how they know.

ASSESSMENT

Working Scientifically

o Em. With support, children identify and match pictures.

o Exp. Children identify and match pictures independently.

o Exc. Children are able to explain reasons for their choices.

Area 2: Opticians

If you invite an optician to talk to the class or you visit an optician, children could help set this area up and include:

o Large interactive picture of the eye with moveable labels for eyebrow, eyelash, iris, pupil, eyelid, etc.

o Optician's eye chart (Activity Resource 1.2), then challenge children to think of other ways to test their eyes.

o A range of spectacles for children to use to look at their surroundings. They could use donated glasses from home, which can be given to charity after the topic.

o A range of items that children can look through, e.g. binoculars, magnifying lenses, periscopes, telescopes, kaleidoscopes, colour paddles, colour mixing glasses, sunglasses, 3D glasses, etc. How do they change what children see?

o Appointment booking form (Activity Resource 1.3) and role play the activity.

o Photographs or pictures of people wearing glasses; include members of school staff and children as well as famous people.

ASSESSMENT

Subject Knowledge

o Em. With support, children talk about the eye and the sense of sight.

o Exp. Children know that they see with their eyes and the sense is sight.

o Exc. Children name different parts of the eye.

Area 3: I am a scientist

o White laboratory coats (white shirts) for children to wear. You could limit these to regulate the number of children using the area.

o Children's goggles or protective glasses to wear to help them take on the role of a scientist.

o X-rays of different parts of the body. These could be stuck on a window so that children can see the detail. You could include pictures of parts of the body for children to match to the X-ray.

o Skeleton models, pictures of skeletons, skeleton jigsaws.

o A range of mirrors, (plain, concave and convex), for children to observe themselves. Children could use the emotion cards (Activity Resource 1.1) and watch themselves show the emotion on the card in the mirror.

o A stethoscope for children to listen to their own and their friend's heartbeat.

o Photographs and posters of scientists and people engaged in science-related jobs, e.g. optician, radiographer, doctor.

ASSESSMENT

Subject Knowledge

o Em. With support, children talk about the different parts of the body.

o Exp. Children can name basic parts of the body.

o Exc. Children name different parts of the human skeleton and compare similarities and differences with other animal skeletons.

1.1 My body

GET STARTED

This is a whole class or group activity to find out what children already know about the human body. Depending on your resources, you could use a human body mat, poster or torso. If you don't have these available, you could give children a body outline (e.g. outline of a child, either drawn on paper or on the playground) and ask them to label different parts of the body and then any bones or other features they already know about, such as their heart.

At this stage, take the majority agreement, which forms an assessment of what children know at the beginning of the topic. You can repeat this at the end to show how learning has changed.

LET'S THINK LIKE SCIENTISTS

Use these questions to develop research skills and speaking and listening:
o What would happen if you did not have a skeleton?
o Which part of your body do you think is the most important?
o Which of the five senses do you think is the most important?
o How are you the same and different to other animals, for example, a cat?

ACTIVITIES

1 MY BODY APRON

L.O. Gather and record data to help answer questions. Identify, name, draw and label the basic parts of the human body.

o Powerpoints slides 1–5 can be used to introduce the topic, revise key words and introduce the apron below.

o Plastic disposable aprons can be purchased in packs of 100 and are great for a range of science activities as the children can draw and label body parts on them such as bones, e.g. ribs, sternum (breast bone) and hips; or the major organs such as the heart, stomach and lungs. Using dry wipe pens, children draw and label parts of the body on an apron. They can then share and compare with others and make changes if they want to. This activity is best carried out during the topic as children learn the different body parts as they go so they can add to the apron over a period of time. Children will love to wear these when they are working in the 'Science Laboratory' or during science sessions and will take ownership of them.

o Do buy disposable aprons for adults working with the children to wear and draw on during topic sessions.

YOU WILL NEED

o PowerPoint Slides 1– 5
o Plastic disposable apron for each child
o Pens to draw on the aprons

ASSESSMENT

Subject Knowledge
o Em. With support, be able to name basic body parts, e.g. arm, leg.
o Exp. Be able to name a wide range of parts of the body, e.g. ankle, wrist.
o Exc. Be able to give some more scientific names for parts of the body, e.g. spine, skull, ribs.

Working Scientifically
o Em. With support be able to use labels to record basic parts of the body.
o Exp. Be able to use, e.g. a word mat, to find correct words to label parts of the body.
o Exc. Be able to label using more scientific language for parts of the body.

② DOG BISCUIT SKELETON

L.O. Gather and record data to help in answering questions. Identify, name, draw and label the basic parts of the human body.

o You can use PowerPoint Slide 6 to introduce this activity.

o For this activity, you will need a set of bone-shaped dog biscuits of different sizes, enough for children working in pairs. Challenge the children to make a human skeleton using the bones. Place children in pairs so that they can discuss which 'bones' to use, where to place them and to share their personal knowledge of the bones and human structure. Extensions to this activity could include:

- Give children books or posters. They can research skeletons and refine their skeleton if they need to.
- Challenge children to label the skeleton with names of the bones, using sticky notes.
- Read *Funnybones*. Leave the book out and challenge children to create 'dog bone' skeletons of the animals in the book, or silly ones, such as the ones made by the Big and Little Skeleton.
- Show them PowerPoint Slide 7 and have them name the animal.
- Search the Internet for images of animal skeletons such as fish, cats, giraffes and put them out for children to copy and make their own dog bone skeletons. Discuss with children the similarities and differences between human and other animals' skeletons, e.g. legs, skull, backbone, fins, neck.

YOU WILL NEED

o PowerPoint Slides 6–7
o Bone-shaped dog biscuits
o Books and posters to research skeletons
o Sticky notes
o Copy of *Funnybones* by Janet and Allan Ahlberg

ASSESSMENT

Subject Knowledge

o Em. With support, children identify bones to show basic body parts.
o Exp. Independently, children identify bones to show basic body parts.
o Exc. Children add additional body parts, e.g. spine, ribs, skull, hips, knee caps.

Working Scientifically

o Em. With support, be able to use labels to record basic parts of the body.
o Exp. Be able to use, e.g. a word mat, to find correct words to label parts of the body.
o Exc. Be able to label using more scientific language for parts of the body.

③ UNDER THE MICROSCOPE

L.O. Identify, name, draw and label the basic parts of the human body
Observe closely, using simple equipment.

o This activity focuses on children using a digital microscope, such as an Easi-Scope, to enable them to closely observe parts of the body, e.g. hair, ears, nose and tongue.

o Show children how to use the microscope (or hand lens). Introduce the items to look at using PowerPoint Slide 8. Try the following activities with children:

- Body parts – leave the 'Parts of my body' cards (Activity Resource 1.4) next to the digital microscope and challenge children to look at the different parts of the body to find out something new or interesting that they could not observe using only their eyes.
- If using a digital microscope, children could take photographs to be printed and place them alongside a large-scale display or model of a child's body with written comments.

YOU WILL NEED

o PowerPoint Slide 8
o Easi-Scope digital microscope and / or hand lenses
o Activity Resource 1.4
o Large-scale display or outline of human body

ASSESSMENT

Subject Knowledge

o Em. With support, children are able to name the part of the body they are observing.
o Exp. Children are able to name the part of the body they are observing.
o Exc. Children are able to name the part of the body they are observing and, if appropriate, talk about which sense it is linked to.

- Challenge children to look at different details, e.g. how many different things do you notice when you look at your skin, your tongue, etc.?

ASSESSMENT

Working Scientifically

o Em. With support, children observe closely using a microscope or hand lens and when prompted describe what they see.

o Exp. Children independently observe and talk about details using a microscope or hand lens.

o Exc. Children choose to extend their observations to compare similarities and differences, e.g. their skin with a friend.

4 THE TALLEST PERSON

L.O. Use observations and ideas to suggest answers to questions.

o The aim of this series of activities is to engage children in comparing themselves with others, using measurements and comparative mathematical language in science. The starting point could be to show them a photograph or video clip of the current record holder of the tallest person. This should provoke a 'wow!' response from children and a stimulus for thinking about themselves and also a model for comparing themselves with other children.

- Prior to the lesson, draw an outline of the tallest person in the UK, who is currently Paul Sturgess at 231 cm tall wearing size 18 shoes. You could draw the outline on the school playground, in the hall or on the back of some wallpaper.

- Children could stand or lie down beside the outline and compare their height to Paul's. Discuss whether they estimate that they could get two of themselves into his outline. Let them try it with a partner.

- Get children to organise themselves in a line beside the outline of Paul, from tallest to shortest, then to lie down on the ground in the same order so that a photograph can be taken of them. Back in the classroom use this to discuss comparisons.

o Next, tell children to organise themselves so that the person next to them draws around them. The aim is to end up with everyone in the class being drawn around so that when they all stand up you have the equivalent of a human graph on the floor for children to think about. Question children as to what this shows so they begin to realise that graphs represent real information. Use the human graph as a starting point for discussion and other activities, e.g.:

- What could you use to measure Paul?

- Working in pairs, how could you measure each other?

- Do you think you are shorter or longer than one of Paul's legs? How could you find out?

- What do you think it would be like to be really tall?

- What would be the useful things about being tall?

- What kind of things would be hard? Would you like to be really tall? Why do you think that?

YOU WILL NEED

o Photo or video clip of the world's tallest person: http://www. guinnessworldrecords.com/world-records/tallest-man-living

http://www.guinnessworldrecords. com/.../yao-defen-worlds-tallest-woman-dies-aged-40-4614

http://easyscienceforkids.com/ all-about-human-bones/

http://kidshealth.org/en/kids/ bones.html

o Chalk or other removable marker for drawing on floor or playground

ASSESSMENT

Working Scientifically

o Em. Children need support to use observations to compare themselves and make sense of the human graph to answer questions.

o Exp. Children use comparative language to make comparisons independently to answer questions.

o Exc. Children use the human graph to suggest and answer their own questions.

1.2 My senses

GET STARTED

Humans have five senses that help them to function. Each sense is important in its own right, but each has its limits so five senses working together is best. You could begin by discussing the senses with children, listing them and providing a picture (e.g. nose, mouth), creating a carousel of activities where children have to choose what they are using to find out about the object, e.g. with a lemon they could be using sight, smell, touch or taste, with a rain stick they could use hearing or sight. In pairs children can discuss and decide which sense they are using.

LET'S THINK LIKE SCIENTISTS

Use these questions to develop research skills and speaking and listening:
- Which sense do you think you use the most?
- Which sense do you think a dog uses the most?
- What would happen if you lost your sense of smell? Which smell would you miss the most?
- Which sense would you like to change into a super sense, and why?

ACTIVITIES: SMELL

SMELL TABLE

L.O. Observe closely, using simple equipment. Say which part of the body is associated with each sense.

- Introduce the topic using PowerPoint Slide 9.
- Create a 'smell table' including items such as scented candles, soaps, potpourri, flavoured biscuits and perfume samples (perhaps a local chemist might provide free samples or almost empty perfume bottles). Don't forget to include some 'less popular smells' too such as vinegar, a smelly sock or a very ripe banana. Change the smells regularly. Encourage children to work with a partner to discuss the smells and which part of the body they are using; talk with children about smell being one of the five senses.

YOU WILL NEED

- PowerPoint Slide 9
- A range of smelly items for your smell table, including less popular smells

ASSESSMENT

Subject Knowledge

- Em. When prompted with questions, children describe the smells and which part of the body they are using.
- Exp. Children use descriptive language to describe the smells and can say that they use their nose to smell.
- Exc. Children compare different smells, independently order them from worst to most pleasant, bring things from the school grounds or home to add to the collection and explain that smell is one of the five senses.

Working Scientifically

- Em. With support to focus on using their sense of smell, children make observations.
- Exp. Children are able to make observations using their sense of smell.
- Exc. Children are able to make comparisons between their observations.

SMELL POTS

L.O. Say which part of the body is associated with each sense.
Using observations and ideas to suggest answers to questions.

o Use PowerPoint Slide 10 to introduce the children to 'smell pots' and tell them they will make their own, some with pleasant smells and some unpleasant. When made, they ask someone else to use their sense of smell to decide what is in the pot. Encourage children not to use this as a guessing game but to think about what they can smell, e.g. 'Where have you smelled this before? Is it a pleasant or an unpleasant smell? Is it a strong smell?'

YOU WILL NEED

o PowerPoint Slide 10
o A range of containers (enough for children to work in pairs or groups)
o Elastic bands
o Fabric such as muslin, curtain net
o A range of items such as apple, bath oil, fabric conditioner, lime, onion, plasticine, vinegar, washing-up liquid, lemon, rose petals, coffee granules, crushed garlic, herbs, orange juice

ASSESSMENT

Subject Knowledge

o Em. With prompt questions, children link the sense of smell with their nose.
o Exp. Children can say that they use their nose to smell.
o Exc. Children explain that smell is one of the five senses.

Working Scientifically

o Em. Children need support to make their smell pots and only guess contents of pots.
o Exp. Children independently make smell pots and describe and name what the smell is in other pots.
o Exc. Children request to use alternative items to make smell pots and offer reasons for their answers to what makes the smell in other pots.

STINKY SOCKS

L.O. Say which part of the body is associated with each sense. Gather and record data to help in answering questions.

o This is a fun alternative to smell pots using dry items with a distinctive smell (see list for examples). Instead of putting smelly items in a pot, children put the items in a sock. Challenge children to work in pairs to make the stinkiest socks, and then ask them to smell each one to find out which is the worst and the best and vote. Collect the votes as a tally chart or a pictogram, asking children to use the data to answer these questions:

• Which smell was the least popular?
• Which smell was the favourite?
• Put the smells in order of least to most popular.
• Why do you think some children chose the least popular? What was the smell like?

YOU WILL NEED

o Old socks (clean)
o Variety of dry smelly objects such as lavender, orange, lemon or lime peel, onion, cheese, different scented soaps

ASSESSMENT

Subject Knowledge

o Em. With prompt questions, children link the sense of smell with their nose.
o Exp. Children can say that they use their nose to smell.
o Exc. Children explain that smell is one of the five senses.

Working Scientifically

o Em. Children require support to make stinky socks, and record and use a tally chart.
o Exp. Children independently make stinky socks, record their data on a given tally chart and can use the data to answer questions.
o Exc. Children make their own tally charts to find out answers to questions.

4 SMELLY HERBS

L.O. Say which part of the body is associated with each sense.
Identify and name a variety of common garden plants. Using their observations and ideas to suggest answers to questions.

o When rubbed, herb plants produce a pungent smell, which some children may recognise, e.g. from eating pizzas or using soap. Discuss with children that herbs are plants; they can be grown, we can eat parts of them and they have a strong smell.

o Tell children to rub leaves between their fingers and, using their sense of smell, ask them if they recognise it and where or when they have smelled it before. Check that children know that they use their noses to smell and we say that this is our sense of smell.

o Compare the scent of dried herbs with fresh herbs. Which do children think smell stronger?

o Children can vote for their favourite herb. Give each child a 'token' (counter) and ask them to identify and name their favourite herb and place their counter next to it. Once counted, the results can be used to create and interrogate a pictogram, as an example of a survey type of enquiry.

o Children can cook with herbs and vote for their favourite, e.g.:

  • oregano and basil on pizza

  • mint in couscous or mint tea

  • chives or parsley in cottage cheese.

YOU WILL NEED

o Herb plants from home, the school garden or a supermarket, e.g. basil, chamomile, chives, coriander (cilantro), curry plant, lavender, lemon balm, marjoram, mint, oregano, rosemary, sage, tarragon and thyme

o A selection of dried herbs

o Counters

ASSESSMENT

Subject Knowledge

o Em. Children can say they can smell things using their nose but do not use the idea of sense of smell confidently. They know that herbs are plants but aren't confident in naming them.

o Exp. Children can say that they have a sense of smell and they use their nose to smell things. They know herbs are plants and can name common ones, e.g. mint.

o Exc. Children use their sense of smell to distinguish between herbs and actively learn the names of a wider range.

Working Scientifically

o Em. With support, children talk about their observations.

o Exp. Children use their observations to suggest ideas and answers to questions.

o Exc. Children use their observations to make links with their subject knowledge, to suggest ideas and to answer their own questions.

5 SMELLS OUTDOORS

L.O. Say which part of the body is associated with each sense.
Observe closely.

o In this activity, children use this sense to find as many things as they can that have a smell. Give groups a camera each to take photographs of things that they can smell. Some groups could video themselves smelling things in the environment, identifying them, naming them and describing the smell. Challenge children to use the scientific vocabulary they have learned, e.g. smell, nose, sense of smell.

YOU WILL NEED

o Camera

o Access to different flowers and plants

ASSESSMENT

Subject Knowledge

o Em. Children smell objects but do not make links with the idea of a sense of smell or they do not link to the nose.

o Exp. Children are able to observe and talk about smell linked to using their nose.

o Exc. Children talk about using their sense of smell.

ACTIVITIES: TASTE

① WHAT'S THAT TASTE?

L.O. Identify and classify. Say which part of the body is associated with each sense.

o Focus on the idea that taste is one of the five senses and that we taste using our mouth. User PowerPoint Slide 10. Ask children to work in pairs; this will provide the opportunity for children to discuss and compare their experiences and share language.

o Ask children to think about why we need to eat different kinds of foods, and not too many sweets and crisps. Have a tasting session using small pieces of different foods. Use the 'Taste me' cards (Activity Resource 1.5) and ask the children to match the taste and texture cards to the food.

o Do introduce new foods to the children, particularly fruits and savoury foods. Take photographs of children tasting – sour tastes result in interesting facial expressions!

YOU WILL NEED

o PowerPoint Slide 11
o Small pieces of different foods, including familiar and unfamiliar tastes. Be careful of any food allergies, e.g. nuts, eggs
o Activity Resource 1.5
o Camera

ASSESSMENT

Subject Knowledge

o Em. Children begin to link the idea of taste as one of the five senses and that we taste using our mouths.
o Exp, Children can say that taste is one of the five senses and know we taste with our mouths.
o Exc. Children go beyond by talking about different kinds of taste, e.g. sweet, sour, bitter.

Working Scientifically

o Em. Children describe what they taste.
o Exp. Children identify the taste, e.g. type of food.
o Exc. Children identify the taste, e.g. sweet, sour, bitter.

② FAVOURITE TASTES

L.O. Gather and record data to help in answering questions.

o An obvious activity but useful for children developing their ability to gather and record data.

o Create the outline of a class pictogram and leave pictures of different foods in pots by the graph. Children choose their favourite and attach it to the graph. Children use the data to answer questions such as:

• Which food is the most popular?
• Which food is the least popular?
• How many more children liked x food than y food?
• How could you do your own favourite food survey at home?
• If you have a parallel Year 1 class, you could swap pictograms so that children answer questions about a different set of data.

YOU WILL NEED

o Large outline of pictogram
o Pictures of different foods (include multiple copies of each food)
o Small pots

ASSESSMENT

Subject Knowledge

o With support, children place data on the pictogram.
o Exp: Children use the pictograph to answer questions.
o Exc. Children are able to ask their own questions using the pictogram.

Working Scientifically

o Em. Children describe what they taste.
o Exp. Children identify the taste, e.g. type of food.
o Exc. Children identify the taste, e.g. sweet, sour, bitter.

❸ TRICKING OUR TASTE BUDS

L.O. Say which part of the body is associated with each sense. Performing simple tests.
Using their observations and ideas to suggest answers to questions.

○ In this activity children use two senses at the same time and find out how one affects the other.

○ Children work in pairs to carry out a simple test where one child is blindfolded (or has eyes closed) and the other identifies the food. Ask children to think about whether or not being able to see the food affects our taste.

○ In the second part of this activity, children taste a piece of apple and a piece of potato. They repeat this and the second time they hold their nose whilst tasting. Ask children to think about whether this affects what they can taste. Do they think that the two senses of smell and taste work together?

○ Ask children to think about what else they would like to try; ask them to use question stems such as 'What if…?':

　• What if I close my eyes and pinch my nose?
　• What if the food is very cold?
　• What if I only use my sense of touch to find out what the food is?

YOU WILL NEED

○ A range of foods for tasting, including pieces of apple and cooked potato

ASSESSMENT

Subject Knowledge

○ Em. Children know which part of the body is linked to taste and smell.

○ Exp. Children know that the senses work together.

○ Exc. Children apply their knowledge of the senses to ask questions and set up tests.

Working Scientifically

○ Em. Children require support to carry out each of the activities.

○ Exp. Children can carry out the test, use their observations to answer questions and know how that the senses work together.

○ Exc. Children do their own tests and use their observations to answer their questions.

ACTIVITIES: SIGHT

❶ MY EYES

L.O. Say which part of the body is associated with each sense.
Gather and record data to help in answering questions.

○ Introduce the topic with PowerPoint Slides 12–13.

○ Give each child a mirror to observe their own eyes. Ask them to draw what they see and label the parts, e.g. *eyelid, eyebrow, eyelash, pupil, iris*.

○ An alternative is to give each child an outline of the eye to label. Then each child indicates their eye colour on a pictograph as a class.

○ When all children have done this, encourage children to say what they notice about the graph, and ask questions about the data, e.g.:

　• How many children have blue, green eyes, etc.?
　• Which is the most common eye colour? Which eye colour is the least common?
　• How many people have the same colour eyes as you?

YOU WILL NEED

○ PowerPoint Slides 12–13
○ Small mirrors
○ Drawing materials and / or outlines of the eye for labelling

ASSESSMENT

Subject Knowledge

○ Em. Children need prompt questions to help them say that they use their eyes to see.

○ Exp. Children know that they see using their eyes to see and this is the sense of sight.

○ Exc. Children can explain that sight is one of the five senses.

Working Scientifically

○ Em. Children are given help to place their data on a pictograph.

- How many more people have blue eyes than hazel, etc.?
- How could we find out if there are more children with blue eyes in Year 2 than in Year 1?

○ Exp. Children record their own data on the pictograph, answer the question using the pictograph and answer given questions.
○ Exc. Children are able to ask and answer their own questions about the data.

② WHY ARE EYES IMPORTANT?

L.O. Say which part of the body is associated with each sense.

○ Ask children what they already know about the senses and what they know about the sense of sight and the eye. Challenge them to learn how to *spell sense, sight* and *eye*. Working in pairs, children could test each other.

○ Using an image of an eye on a display or interactive whiteboard, display children's responses to why their eyes are important. What would they miss the most if they were unable to see? What are their favourite things to see?

YOU WILL NEED

○ Images or outlines of the eye
○ Photographs of various objects

ASSESSMENT

Subject Knowledge

○ Em. Children can say that they see with their eyes, but are unsure of the word *sight* and are unable to spell associated words.
○ Exp. Children know what sight is and can spell associated words.
○ Exc. Children are able to record their responses in sentences using and spelling sight vocabulary correctly.

③ SENSING WITHOUT SIGHT

L.O. Say which part of the body is associated with each sense.

○ The following choice of activities allow children to explore what it would be like not to have sight.

○ In pairs, one child blindfolded (or with eyes closed) and the other supporting, ask children to find out what is on their tables using all their senses except sight. One child offers unusual textures, e.g. pine cones, and brushes or slimy things, e.g. tapioca and porridge. Include objects that make sounds, e.g. xylophone, bell, baby's rattle.

○ Create a dark area either in the classroom (e.g. using blackout material draped over a table) or take the class into a room that can be blacked out and ask children what they can see.

○ Working in pairs, one child should be blindfolded or wearing blacked-out goggles while the other child takes them for a walk. The unhindered child should carefully guide their partner around the school grounds using language to describe where to go and obstacles. Children then compare how they felt when they cannot see where they are going, e.g. frightened, unsteady, unsure.

○ Invite a sight-impaired visitor to talk with the class about their daily lives, to show what they use to assist them and that they can carry out daily tasks, etc.

YOU WILL NEED

○ Large blanket or blackout material
○ Blindfolds or blacked-out goggles
○ Objects with a range of textures or that make sounds (examples given with activity instructions)

ASSESSMENT

Subject Knowledge

○ Em. Children require support to link the sense of sight with eyes.
○ Exp. Children can say that the sense of sight is linked to their eyes.
○ Exc. Children recognise how the different senses are linked.

④ WHAT IS IT?

L.O. Observe closely, using simple equipment.

o Children look closely at objects around the school grounds and take photographs from interesting angles to create a 'Guess what it is' board. Alternatively, they could use a digital microscope to take photographs of an object close up. They discuss with partners the photographs and make suggestions.

YOU WILL NEED

o Camera or digital microscope

ASSESSMENT

Working Scientifically

o Em. Children require support with observations and using equipment.

o Exp. Independently, they use equipment to take photographs.

o Exc. They make decisions about what equipment to use to observe closely, take photographs and explain why.

⑤ MATCH THE EYES

L.O. Describe and compare the structure of a variety of common animals. Identify and classify.

o Give children pictures of animals along with a set of pictures showing only the eyes of animals and challenge them to match the eyes to the correct animal. Ask children to talk about the eyes, e.g. shape, colour, size, position, and compare with other animals including themselves.

YOU WILL NEED

o Pictures of animals

o Pictures of same animals showing just their eyes

ASSESSMENT

Subject Knowledge

o Em. Children need support to describe the eyes.

o Exp. Children are able to describe and compare the different eyes.

o Exc. Children research other animals and describe and compare different animal eyes.

Working Scientifically

o Em. Children are supported to identify the animal.

o Exp. Children can identify the animal.

o Exc. Children can explain how they used different features to identify the animal.

⑥ KIM'S GAME

L.O. Say which part of the body is associated with each sense.
Observe closely.

o The aim of this activity is for children to observe carefully and remember which items were placed in front of them. They close their eyes whilst an object is removed from a collection. Then, working with their partner or in a small group, they say which item has been removed. You could use this activity at different times of the years varying the items accordingly, e.g. science equipment, fruits and vegetables, leaves, flowers. During the activity, talk about which of the five senses they are using to reinforce this idea.

YOU WILL NEED

o A range of objects to memorise, which could be related or random

ASSESSMENT

Subject Knowledge

o Em. Children can say which sense they use, but might need support and fewer items to recall.

o Exp. Children know which sense they are using.

o Exc. Children are able to say which of the five senses they are using.

Working Scientifically

o Em. Children may require fewer items to observe and recall.

o Exp. Children focus their observations on finding a missing item.

o Exc. Children develop a group strategy to use observations to find missing items.

HELPING US TO SEE BETTER?

L.O. Observe closely, using simple equipment.

o Allow children to use and explore a range of optical equipment such as binoculars, a telescope and a microscope, so they begin to understand how some items are useful to help us see things that are far away or that are very small. Encourage them to work in pairs and discuss how the different equipment changes what they see.

YOU WILL NEED

o Optical equipment including magnifying glass, binoculars, telescope and microscope

ASSESSMENT

Working Scientifically

o Em. With support, children use equipment to make observations.

o Exp. Children use the equipment independently and talk about what they can see.

o Exc. Children are able to choose the correct equipment for the job and talk about the differences between using it and only using their eyes.

ACTIVITIES: TOUCH

USING MY HANDS

L.O. Say which part of the body is associated with each sense.
Identify and name a variety of everyday materials, including wood, plastic, glass, metal, water and rock. Identify and classify.

o Introduce the topic using PowerPoint Slides 14–15.

o Lay out a variety of materials with different textures for children to pick up and feel. Allow the children to explore what they are feeling with their hands; this links well with learning about different materials.

o Focus on their understanding of touch as one of the five senses and that we use our hands to find out what things are like.

o Help to develop their vocabulary by encouraging them to say what the material may be made from and ask them to describe what things feel like and introduce words such as:

- *texture, feel*
- *smooth, rough*
- *warm, cold*
- *silky, squidgy*
- *wet, hard*
- *bumpy, sticky*

YOU WILL NEED

o PowerPoint Slides 14–15

o Samples of materials, possibly including shaving cream, rock, instant snow powder, jelly, pine cones, sandpaper, soil, cotton wool, metal, fabric, broken crackers, wood, plastic

ASSESSMENT

Subject Knowledge

o Em. Children know they are using their hands to feel things and describe textures.

o Exp. Children know they are using their hands and this is their sense of touch. They can use scientific vocabulary to describe textures.

o Exc. Children know that the sense of touch is one of the five senses and can use scientific vocabulary to describe textures.

o Exc. Children are able to compare materials and their textures using scientific vocabulary.

Working Scientifically

o Em. With support, children name different materials.

o Exp. Children are able to identify different materials.

o Exc. Children are able to apply their knowledge of materials to classify their observations.

2 NAMING PARTS OF MY HANDS

L.O. Identify, draw and label basic parts of the human body and say which part of the body is associated with each sense.

o Start by reminding children that touch is one of the five senses. Ask each child to draw around their own hand on paper large enough to add labels. With their partner, they talk about the parts of the hand that they know, e.g. *fingertips, nails, thumb*. Scaffold new words such as *knuckle, little finger and palm*; provide words to use as labels around their hand.

YOU WILL NEED

o Drawing materials
o Labels of parts of the hand

ASSESSMENT

Subject Knowledge

o Em. Children know that hands are used to touch but are unsure of the names of different parts of the hand.
o Exp. Children know touch is one of the five senses and can label some parts of the hand.
o Exc. Children know the five senses and can label all the different parts of the hand.

3 FEELY PICTURE

L.O. Say which part of the body is associated with each sense.

o Explain to children that they are going to make a 'feely picture' so that they can use their sense of touch.

o Provide children with a wide range of fabrics and other materials to make their 'feely picture', e.g. if they are creating a cat they might use a soft, fluffy material or for a tree trunk they might use sandpaper.

YOU WILL NEED

o A range of fabrics or materials with different textures

ASSESSMENT

Subject Knowledge

o Em. With support, children link the sense of touch with feeling different textures.
o Exp. Children choose different textures that are appropriate for their 'feely picture'.
o Exc. Children choose materials to create different textures on their picture.

4 WHICH IS BEST?

L.O. Say which part of the body is associated with each sense.
Perform simple tests.

o Ask children to use different parts of their body, other than their hands, to touch different materials and texture, e.g. touching objects using their elbows and feet. This investigation looks at the following question: 'Are other parts of the body more or less sensitive than our hands?'

o Ask children to work with a partner to think about what kind of simple test they could do to find the answer to this question. For instance, they could collect materials with different textures and make observations using touch, feeling them using their hands, feet, elbows or cheeks. They should use their experience to answer the question.

YOU WILL NEED

o A range of materials with different textures

ASSESSMENT

Subject Knowledge

o Em. With support, children link the sense of touch with feeling different textures.
o Exp. Children choose different textures for their test.
o Exc. Children answer the question linking their observations to the sense used

Working Scientifically

o Em. Children use verbal or pictorial support to plan and carry out this activity.
o Exp. With some support, children plan and carry out this simple test and can answer the question.
o Exc. Independently, children plan, carry out the test and answer the question.

ACTIVITIES: HEARING

1 USING OUR EARS TO HEAR

L.O. Say which part of the body is associated with each sense. Use observations and ideas to suggest answers to questions.

- Introduce the topic using PowerPoint Slide 16.

- Give children a mirror so that they can look at and link the senses of taste, smell and sight to parts of their face. Ask children to point to and say which part of their head they use to hear; most children should find this very easy. Write the word *hear* so that ear can be picked out. Explain that if they learn to spell the word *hear* they can also spell *ear*.

- Get children to look at their ears and talk about the ear lobe. Warn them not to put anything inside their ear or make loud sounds.

- Children could make a headband with 'big ears' and wear them on a 'listening walk' around the school, both indoors and outdoors. Tell children that their new ears might help them to hear more sounds.

- To record this activity children could use a tally chart and take photographs of what they can hear to contribute to a class list.

YOU WILL NEED

- PowerPoint Slide 16
- Mirrors
- Materials to make a headband with big ears
- Camera

ASSESSMENT

Subject Knowledge

- Em. With support, children can point to and name their ears.
- Exp. Children point to and name the ear and say that they can hear with it.
- Exc. Children confidently talk about what they can hear with their ears and how to look after them.

Working Scientifically

- Em. Children describe their observations.
- Exp. Children use their observations to answer questions about the sounds they hear.
- Exc. Children use scientific language when answering questions about sounds they hear, e.g. sense, hearing, ears, high, low.

2 WHERE IS THE SOUND?

L.O. Perform simple tests.

- In this activity, the class carries out a simple test to find out if children can move without being heard. Tell children that they are going to carry out a simple test to find out who can move quietly and not be caught. This could be a whole class activity where children form a circle and a child stands in the middle, blindfolded or with hands over eyes. The rest of the children stay quiet and, for example, a teddy bear is passed from child to child. The child in the middle shouts 'stop!' and the child holding the teddy bear speaks using a silly voice. The blindfolded child has to point in the right direction of the one who spoke in the silly voice.

- A variation on this is to place an object, such as a bunch of keys, beside a child on the floor and another child from the surrounding circle has to creep across the floor to try to pick up the object. The child in the middle has to point to where they hear any sounds and, if they are correct, the 'creeper' has to go back and someone else is chosen. The child who picks up the keys without being heard can then take the place in the middle.

YOU WILL NEED

- Blindfold
- Toys or objects such as keys to pass around or collect

ASSESSMENT

Working Scientifically

- Em. Children need support in understanding and carrying out this simple test.
- Exp. Children confidently participate in this test.
- Exc. Children note where a test is incorrect or make suggestions for improvements.

③ MATCH THE SOUND

L.O. Say which part of the body is associated with each sense. Observing closely.

We often think of observation as being only using sight, but we can observe using all of the senses and, in this activity, children use the sense of hearing.

- Using small opaque containers with materials in them, make sure that the containers are paired so that, if there is rice in one container, there is another container with the same amount of rice.
- Children work with a partner to pair up the containers by listening to the sound they make when shaken.
- This can be made more challenging by working in the hall or outdoors where each child has a container and has to listen to others' containers to find the one that matches theirs.
- You could extend this activity by giving children sets of empty containers for them to recreate this activity to play with another group.

YOU WILL NEED

- A class set of small opaque containers with lids and containing a range of materials, e.g. feathers, buttons, pasta, a stone or pieces of fabric

ASSESSMENT

Subject Knowledge

- Em. Children know that they hear with their ears but need support in using this sense to listen carefully to distinguish sounds.
- Exp. Children know that they hear with their ears and that hearing is one of the five senses. They observe closely to distinguish between sounds.
- Exc. Children are able to distinguish between sounds, can describe them and talk about what makes the sounds and why.

Let's think like scientists

SWITCHED ON
Science
Second Edition

Sense of hearing

If you could not hear things, what would you miss the most?

Why do you think we have two ears instead of just one ear?

© Monika Wisniewska / Adobe Stock

TOPIC 2 Celebrations

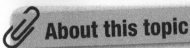
About this topic

Curriculum link: Year 1, Animals, including humans

SUMMARY:

This topic uses the theme of celebrations to explore a number of curriculum areas, including everyday materials, plants and light. There are a number of activities to choose from, all offering opportunities for cross-curricular work.

UNITS:

2.1: Our celebration: light

2.2: Our celebration: music

2.3: Our celebration: food

ACTIVITY RESOURCES:

• 2.1: Hand shadows

• 2.2: Bottle top clackers

• 2.3: Kazoo

• 2.4: Ice cube tray xylophone

• 2.5: Tin can drums

• 2.6: Are you ready to cook?

• 2.7: Charoset

• 2.8: Chinese spring rolls

• 2.9: Stuffed dates   • 2.10: Christingle

ONLINE RESOURCES:

Teaching slides (Powerpoint) : Celebrations

Interactive activity: Celebrations

CPD video: Celebrations

Pupil video: Celebrations

Word mat: Celebrations

Editable Planning: Celebrations

Topic Test: Celebrations

Learning objectives

This topic covers the following learning objectives:

○ Say which part of the body is associated with each sense.

○ Distinguish between an object and the material from which it is made.

○ Identify and name a variety of everyday materials, including wood, plastic, glass, metal, water and rock.

○ Describe the simple physical properties of a variety of everyday materials.

○ Identify and describe the basic structure of a variety of common plants, including trees.

Working scientifically skills

This topic develops the following working scientifically skills:

○ Observe things using simple equipment.

○ Identify and classify.

○ Perform simple tests.

○ Use observations and ideas to suggest answers to questions. Gather and record data to help in answering questions.

CROSS-CURRICULAR LINKS

This topic offers the following cross-curricular opportunities:

English

○ Children re-tell their own experiences of celebrations, write sentences, use Easi-Speak microphones, etc.

○ Plan a party: design and make invitations, choose presents, prepare food and produce entertainment for the whole class and possibly parents and carers.

○ Comparative words, e.g. *bright, brighter, brightest*.

○ Read and follow instructions. Learn and recite a poem linked to celebrations.

○ Re-tell stories or role play a celebrations story, e.g. Rama and Sita (Hindu).

Numeracy and mathematics

○ Measure cooking ingredients for celebration recipes using non-standard and standard measurements.

○ Compare weights when cooking.

○ Use language relating to weeks and months.

Music

○ Music from different kinds of celebrations.

○ Play instruments used in different celebrations.

○ Make and use musical instruments.

Drama and dance
o Re-enact stories.
o Script and perform a shadow puppet play.
o Explore emotions.

RE
o Understand celebrations from world religions.
o What is common between different celebrations?
o Children share their experiences, bring in photographs, special clothes, gifts.
o How do we celebrate in our class and school?

Computing / ICT
o Use Paint program to draw celebration colour explosions, e.g. fireworks.
o Use digital cameras to take photographs.
o Use publishing package to make a celebration card.

Design and technology
o Design, make and use musical instruments, masks, candle holders.
o Design and make puppets, e.g. using wooden spoons, felt puppets, card puppets with dowel.
o Design and make a theatre, e.g. cardboard box.

Art
o Diwali Rangoli patterns using chalk or coloured sand – outdoors.
o Weaving, e.g. paper plate weaving.
o Marbling – celebration colours, for wrapping paper.
o Stamping using different foods to make celebration patterns, e.g. okra, potato, apple.
o Make a Christingle.
o Design and make celebration banners.

History
o Historical stories behind celebrations. Timeline of family celebrations, e.g. birthdays, wedding anniversaries, Christenings.
o Timeline to show when light is used in personal and family celebrations in children's lives.
o History of lights, e.g. candles, gas lamps, electric lights – using a timeline.

Geography
o Celebrations from around the world. Different celebrations and the country, e.g. Diwali and India.
o Using maps to find countries.
o Organisers of local celebrations.
o Food from different cultures eaten during celebrations.
o Celebratory language and greetings in other countries, e.g. Happy New Year in Chinese: 'Kung Hey Fay Choy'.

 ## STEAM (SCIENCE TECHNOLOGY ENGINEERING ART AND MATHS) OPPORTUNITIES

Invite into class
o People from different communities to talk about their celebrations, the senses and food.
o Local fire officers – safety during celebrations, e.g. fireworks.
o Poets and storytellers to use and develop descriptive language linked to the senses, light and dark, material, etc.

Visit
o A supermarket to find out about different fruits and vegetables.

 ## HEALTH AND SAFETY

In this topic, lighted candles are used. This should be under adult supervision and checks relating to setting off smoke alarms should be made. See current *ASE Be Safe!* book for further safety advice. Some activities include cooking and tasting food. Check for children with specific allergies and follow guidance for cooking in science in *ASE Be Safe!* book.

SUBJECT KNOWLEDGE

Light
Whilst the topic Light does not appear in the National Curriculum it is used here as a context for working scientifically and to provide a bridge between children's experiences in EYFS and Year 3. Many celebrations during the autumn and winter months have the theme of light. You could begin

this activity by setting up a table full of different kinds of candles: tall, short, thin, thick, birthday, night lights, etc. For greater impact, and if possible, darken the room and light the candles before children enter.

Shadows

The aim of this series of activities is to help children understand how shadows are made. At this level, children are not required to know that light travels in straight lines, even though it is an important and helpful idea. Because of this, when it hits an object, e.g. a child, light cannot get through, so the area behind is less well-lit and a shadow is formed. The shadow is the same shape as the object (the child) blocking the light. When children make shadows in the following set of activities, encourage them to explain how they think the shadow is made.

 FOOD AND OUR SENSES

Foods vary according to the celebration and the culture. These examples have been chosen to develop children's understanding of key scientific ideas. Once children have tried out the recipes here, they can decide what to make for their own celebration.

'Are you ready to cook?' (Activity Resource 2.6) can be laminated and used repeatedly. The cookery recipes are for children to use under the supervision of an adult. When using the recipes with a group, the aim is for children to work independently. The role of the adult is to focus observation and discussion on some key scientific ideas.

 SCIENTIFIC VOCABULARY: CELEBRATIONS

It is assumed that most children know, from their EYFS experience, words such as *sound, light, eyes* and *ears*, although they might not know how to write and spell them. You can download a Word mat of essential vocabulary for this topic from *My Rising Stars*.

illuminate: brighten up with light

light source: something that gives out light

opaque: a material that does not let light pass through

reflect: when light hits an object and bounces off

translucent: a material that lets some light through but you cannot see through it clearly

transparent: a material that lets light through and you can see things very clearly through it

shadow: the dark shape that an object makes, e.g. on the ground, when it is between the light source (e.g. a torch) and the surface (e.g. the ground)

sound: a vibration that travels through the air and can be heard by the ear

source of sound: an object that makes a sound

vibration: sounds can be made by vibrating an object; something that moves backwards and forwards

key words: bark / battery / bright / bulb / candle / cool / dark / dull / fast / flame / flower / fruit / high / hot / leaf / leaves / light / liquid / loud / low / mirror / observe / plant / quiet / root / senses / shoot / slow / solid / texture / torch / wax / wick

PREPARE THE CLASSROOM

Area 1: Science laboratory
- Lab coats (white shirts) and goggles
- Pictures of scientists, including scientists at work
- Sound makers
- Torches and objects for shadow making
- Kaleidoscopes
- Electric circuit resources, e.g. batteries, bulbs, wires
- Mirrors
- Glow sticks, fibre optic torches

Area 2: Chinese restaurant
- Chinese lanterns
- Menus with photographs
- Paper plates with different meals painted on them
- Chopsticks
- Pieces of food to eat with chopsticks

- Chinese writing / characters on display
- Pictures or models of Chinese dragons

Area 3: Festival outside area
- Dressing-up clothes
- Large pieces of fabric, e.g. to make a Chinese New Year dragon
  - Musical instruments, MP3 or CD player
  - Masks, e.g. animals
  - Sound makers, e.g. rain sticks
  - Cameras
  - Recording Pegs, Easi-Speak microphones

Area 4: Shadow theatre
- Shadow puppets
- Object for making shadows
- White backdrop, e.g. wall, card, sheet
- Torches

2.1 Our celebration: light

GET STARTED

Introduce the topic using Powerpoints 1–4. This is a whole class or group activity to find out what children already know about celebrations. Use PowerPoint Slide 5 to talk about Celebrations. It would also be helpful here to show children a video clip of different celebrations to scaffold children's thinking. With the children, create a mind map scribing what they say and alongside each statement place the child's name to support formative assessment and provide ownership. Children might mention decorations, fairy lights or candles. If not, ask if they know of celebrations that have lots of lights. They might also talk about music and sound, as well as food. Collect their ideas on these areas, which are themes for science activities in this topic.

LET'S THINK LIKE SCIENTISTS

Use these questions to develop research skills and speaking and listening:

o What would it be like if all the lights went out where you live?

o What do you think it would be like without the Sun to give us light?

o If there was a power cut and there was no electricity and the lights at home did not work, what could you use to read or move about your house?

ACTIVITIES: LIGHT

❶ INTRODUCING CANDLES

L.O. Say which part of the body is associated with each sense. Observing closely.

o Set up a table full of candles. Ask children to think about the similarities and differences they can see between the candles.

o Ask them to talk with their friend about what they notice using their senses. Some children might need to be supported by the adult, prompting their observations and thinking by asking:

- What do you see, smell and hear?

- How do the candle flames move? Why do you think that happens?

- Which candle seems to give out the most light?

o Collect statements from children and note any use of key language such as *candle, light, flame, light source, heat.*

o Help children to link the idea that without light we cannot see and that the word *dark* means that there is no light. Ask children when they have been in the dark, what it was like and if they could see anything at all (see Activity 4 'In the dark, dark cave' to help clarify the misconception many children have that you can see in the dark!).

o Take this opportunity to ask them to think about which celebrations they have been involved in or seen, where lights have been important, e.g. 5th November, Christmas, birthdays, Christenings, Chanukah, Diwali, Chinese New Year. At this stage, you might like to go back to the video showing different celebrations, focusing on different light sources. Children could shout out 'light source' as soon as they spot one.

YOU WILL NEED

o A range of candles with different, shapes, colours and scents

ASSESSMENT

Subject Knowledge

o Em. Some children with support can name the senses and parts of the body.

o Exp. Children can say which senses they are using, with which part of the body.

o Exc. Children talk about the five senses and which sense they are using.

Working Scientifically

o Em. Children describe what they see.

o Exp. Children describe their observations and which part of the body they are using to observe.

o Exc. Children apply their subject knowledge to their observations to ask their own questions.

② OBSERVING A CANDLE

L.O. Observe closely. Use their observations and ideas to suggest answers to questions.

o With a small group of children, light a candle and, to be safe, place it in a tray of sand. Discuss the importance of working safely when using candles in the classroom.

o Ask children to think about what other rules might be important around candles, e.g. hair tied back, no loose clothing, do not touch (see *ASE Be Safe!*).

o Encourage children to observe the candle closely and to discuss what they see with others in the group. Use Powerpoints slides 5–7 if you wish. Prompt observations by asking questions such as:

- What is the candle like before it is lit, when it is alight (burning) and when it has been put out (extinguished)?
- What are the different parts of the candle called, e.g. *wax*, *wick*, *flame*?
- What can you see, e.g. colours, movement, shape, size, changes?
- What can you smell and hear?
- What happens if you blow gently on the candle flame? Why does this happen?
- What happens to the wax as the candle burns? Scaffold language by using words such as *melt*, *hot*, *liquid*, *cool*, *solid*.
- Is the candle a source of light?

o Reinforce the idea that a candle is a source of light. Ask children to think about what else is a source of light. They could choose from a set of pictures.

YOU WILL NEED

o PowerPoint Slides 5–7
o Candle
o A tray of sand to put the candle in safely
o Pictures of other light sources

ASSESSMENT

Working Scientifically

o Em. With support, children observe the candle and answer questions.
o Exp. Children independently use their observations to answer questions.
o Exc. Children ask their own questions based on their observations.

③ BRIGHT, BRIGHTER, BRIGHTEST

L.O. Identify and classify.

o Use PowerPoint Slide 8 to introduce the topic.

o Comparative language in science is important and is linked to children's observations. Give children a collection of objects (or pictures) some of which are light sources and others that are not light sources, e.g. torches. Ask children to sort them into two groups: sources of light / not sources of light.

o Then ask children to think about putting the light sources into order using the comparative language:

Bright   Brighter   Brightest

YOU WILL NEED

o PowerPoint Slide 8
o A range of light sources, or pictures of light sources

ASSESSMENT

Working Scientifically

o Em. Some children will need support to identify light sources and place them into the correct set.
o Exp. Children independently identify and sort light sources correctly.
o Exc. Children can explain their reasons for their classifications.

4 IN THE DARK, DARK CAVE

L.O. Using their observations and ideas to suggest answers to questions.

o Ask children to think about how they could make a dark area in the classroom. Give them a range of materials to choose from, and help them to build their dark cave. You need to make sure that you can create a completely dark place, perhaps with some blackout curtain material or with a heavy dark fabric over the top of a couple of desks, with some cushions inside (for comfort).

o Children visit their cave using torches. Each day hide new objects for children to look for, e.g. shiny objects, dark coloured objects or reflective materials.

o Encourage children to think about:
  - What does dark mean? What does dark feel like?
  - How can we see in the dark? What do we need?
  - Which objects do we see first when we shine a light in the cave? (Children might talk about shiny objects or light-coloured objects.)

YOU WILL NEED

o PowerPoint Slide 9
o Material to create a dark area of classroom, e.g. blackout material
o Torches
o Different objects (outlined in activity instructions)

ASSESSMENT

Working Scientifically

o Em. Children need support in using their experience to make sense of and answer questions.

o Exp. Children use their observations to talk about dark and what they can see in their cave.

o Exc. Independently, children choose their own materials for the cave and their own objects to find out which can be seen in their dark area.

ACTIVITIES: SHADOW

1 SHADOW SHAPES

L.O. Perform simple tests.
Use their observations and ideas to suggest answers to questions.

o Make sure that children have a torch with a strong beam. Ask them to test different materials and objects from around the room to see which ones make a shadow, perhaps on a wall or piece of card.

o Introduce children to the words *transparent*, *translucent* and *opaque*. You could use transparent plastic beakers and bottles or translucent tracing paper to see what happens to light and how it is different to opaque objects.

o What do they notice about the object and the shadow? Tell them that they will be asked to show their favourite shadow to other children and explain how they think the shadow is made.

YOU WILL NEED

o PowerPoint Slides 10–11
o Torch
o Objects to cast shadows

ASSESSMENT

Working Scientifically

o Em. Children, with support, can test different things to make a shadow and describe their observations.

o Exp. Children are able to plan and carry out tests to make shadows and use their observations to answer questions.

o Exc. Children are confident in testing and ask further questions, test and suggest answers.

② HAND SHADOWS

L.O. Observe closely.
Describe the simple physical properties of a variety of everyday materials.
Use their observations and ideas to suggest answers to questions.

o In this activity, children explore making shadows and observe closely to find out how what they do affects their shadows and are able to say that opaque materials make shadows. They use their observations to suggest answers to their questions and to ask new ones about making shadows. Whilst children are working, ask them to say what they are trying to find out and what they are doing to answer their question. Using 'Hand shadows' (Activity Resource 2.1), children work in pairs, one child making the shapes with their hands and the other shining the torch. Then children change roles.

o Encourage children to explore making hand shapes of their own and share them with the rest of the class.

YOU WILL NEED

o Activity Resource 2.1
o Torch

ASSESSMENT

Subject Knowledge

o Em. Children can describe what they do to make a shadow.
o Exp. Children describe how a shadow is made using scientific language, e.g. *shadow, opaque*.
o Exc. Children use what they know about shadows and materials to make different shadow effects, e.g. colour, patterns.

Working Scientifically

o Em. Children observe how shadows are made to answer questions.
o Exp. Children use observations and knowledge of materials to answer questions.
o Exc. Children apply knowledge of shadows and materials to ask their own questions and carry out simple tests to answer them.

③ MAKE A SHADOW PUPPET PLAY

L.O. Distinguish between an object and the material from which it is made.

o You could read or tell a story and give children the opportunity to choose from and use a range of materials and resources to re-tell the story as a shadow puppet play they could perform to an audience.

o Include materials such as, paper doilies, which create beautiful, shadow patterns when a light is shone on them. Add coloured cellophane, which creates a colour effect, and provide transparent and translucent materials and dowelling for children to use to hold the shadow puppets. As children work, ask them why they have chosen the materials, e.g. for colour, being see-through, etc. Use Powerpoints 12–14 to illustrate the puppets.

YOU WILL NEED

o PowerPoint Slides 12–14
o Torch
o Materials to make shadow puppets including: paper doilies, coloured cellophane, transparent and translucent materials, dowelling (to hold the puppets)

ASSESSMENT

Subject Knowledge

o Em. With support, children can name what they are using (e.g. lolly stick) to make their shadow puppet.
o Exp. Children can say which material the object they are using is made from.
o Exc. Children choose specific materials based on their properties, e.g. opaque.

2.2 Our celebration: music

GET STARTED

Encourage children to think about how people use different materials in a celebration. When they plan their own celebration, how will they use the different materials to show what they are celebrating?

LET'S THINK LIKE SCIENTISTS

Use these questions to develop research skills and speaking and listening:

o What is your favourite musical instrument? What do you have to do to make it sound?

o What kind of musical instrument could you make using a plastic bottle?

o How does music make you feel? Do different kinds of music make you feel different? How?

ACTIVITIES

❶ BOTTLE TOP CLACKERS

L.O. Describe the simple properties of a variety of everyday materials.

o Look at 'Bottle top clackers' (Activity Resource 2.2 and PowerPoint Slide 15) and work out how they are made. Ask your local restaurant to save bottle tops for the class to use. Ask children to name the materials and why they are useful for making this sound, e.g. the metal is hard and makes a good sound when hit.

YOU WILL NEED

o PowerPoint Slide 15
o Activity Resource 2.2
o Bottle tops and cardboard

ASSESSMENT

Subject Knowledge

o Em. With support, children describe what the materials are made from and are like, e.g. hard.

o Exp. Children make and test their own bottle top clackers and say why bottle tops work.

o Exc. Children make and test their own clackers and can use scientific language to explain how it works and why the materials have been used.

❷ KAZOO

**L.O. Describe the simple properties of a variety of everyday materials.
Perform simple tests.**

o Look at 'Kazoo' (Activity Resource 2.3) and then help children make their own. Demonstrate humming into the end of the kazoo and allow children to play theirs. Explain that the material (usually greaseproof paper) vibrates when they hum into it, which causes the sound to be amplified. The cylinder increases this amplification so the sound is made louder.

o Ask children to think about which other materials could be used to make a kazoo and test their ideas by making and playing them. Are some materials better than others? Why?

YOU WILL NEED

o Activity Resource 2.3
o Greaseproof paper
o Elastic bands
o Cylinder

ASSESSMENT

Subject Knowledge

o Em. Children can name the material used but they require support to say why they are using the material.

o Exp. Children can say why they are using the material, e.g. hard so it makes a certain sound.

o Exc. Children choose materials according to their properties.

Working Scientifically

o Em. With help, children describe what they did to play the kazoo.

o Exp. Children make and test their own kazoo and say which material was best.

o Exc. Children make and test their own kazoo and explain why one material was better than another.

ICE CUBE TRAY XYLOPHONE

L.O. Perform simple tests.

o In this activity, children use ice cube trays as a xylophone. Use Activity Resource 2.4 and give children the opportunity to explore making sounds using beaters made from different materials, e.g. metal and wooden spoons. Sounds are made by hitting or dragging the mallet or beater, which causes the tray to vibrate.

o Ask children to think about how they could change the sounds made; they might suggest using different beaters, different sides and even freezing water to create ice cubes to hit.

o Provide opportunities for children to test their ideas.

YOU WILL NEED

o Activity Resource 2.4
o Ice cube trays
o Metal and wooden beaters

ASSESSMENT

Working Scientifically

o Em. With support, children test different ways to make sounds.

o Exp. Children independently test their ideas.

o Exc. Children test their ideas and extend by suggesting other ways to make a xylophone.

 TIN CAN DRUMS

L.O. Describe the simple properties of a variety of everyday materials.

Perform simple tests.

o Introduce the topic using PowerPoint Slide 16

o Show children 'Tin can drums' (Activity Resource 2.5) and provide them with containers made from different materials so they can make their own drums. As children use their drums, ask them to say which material the drum is made from and why it is useful as a drum, e.g. hard, makes a specific sound.

o Ask children to test the 'drums' made from different materials, e.g. card, plastic, wood, metal. Which material makes the best drum for them? There is no correct answer here because it will depend on what kind of sound children like best.

o Encourage them to say what they like about their drum and the sound.

YOU WILL NEED

o PowerPoint Slide 16
o Activity Resource 2.5
o Empty containers made from different materials including metal, wood, plastic, card
o Drumsticks made from different materials

ASSESSMENT

Subject Knowledge

o Em. Children can name the material used but they require support to say why they are using the material.

o Exp. Children can say why they are using the material e.g. hard so it makes a certain sound.

o Exc. Children choose materials according to their properties.

Working Scientifically

o Em. With help, children describe what they did to play their drum.

o Exp. Children make and test their own drum, compare different materials and say why they chose that material.

o Exc. Children make and test their own drum and can explain why one material was better than another.

2.3 Our celebration: food

GET STARTED

Have a celebration 'Food taster' activity where children taste bite-size pieces of a range of food. They can keep their own tally chart to show which food they liked and disliked, or match the main ingredient to each food. Encourage children to talk with their partner about the foods and suggest they use words such as *sweet, sour, crunchy, chewy*. To find out which words they are using and which they are unsure of, you could include different fruits and vegetables as well as cooked foods. NB Be careful about allergies and cultural norms.

LET'S THINK LIKE SCIENTISTS

Use these questions to develop research skills and speaking and listening:
o Why do you think there are different kinds of food?
o What do you think it would be like if we all ate only one kind of food?
o What if we could not cook using heat? What kinds of foods would you miss?

ACTIVITIES

WHICH PART OF THE PLANT IS IT?

L.O. Identify and describe the basic structure of a variety of common flowering plants.

o Begin by showing children different fruits and vegetables. Encourage children to use all of their senses to observe the food and talk about which part of a plant an ingredient is, e.g. *leaf, flower, stalk (stem), root*.

o Examples could include:
  - **Fruits:** apples, lemons, raisins (dried grapes), bell peppers, dates (from date palm tree)
  - **Seed pods:** okra, runner beans
  - **Bark:** cinnamon is from the bark of cinnamon trees, rolled into cinnamon sticks or ground into powder
  - **Flowers:** honey is the nectar from the flowers of plants. Bees collect and store it in their hives, where it is changed into the sweet, thick sugary solution. Also cauliflower
  - **Roots:** carrots, sweet potatoes, yam
  - **Shoots:** bean sprouts, spring onions, bamboo shoots
  - **Stem:** celery
  - **Leaves:** cabbage, Chinese lettuce

YOU WILL NEED

o Fruit, seeds, bark, flowers, roots, shoots, stem, leaves: see list of examples in the activity instructions

ASSESSMENT

Subject Knowledge
o Em. With support, children can name some vegetables and know that they come from plants.
o Exp. Children know that the fruits and vegetables given come from plants and can name parts of plants, e.g. root, stem.
o Exc. Children can name a wide range of fruits and vegetables and know which part of the plant they are.

Working Scientifically
o Em. Children match fruits and vegetables to pictures and words.
o Exp. Children use experience to identify and name different fruits and vegetables and plant parts.
o Exc. Children apply subject knowledge to identify and classify fruits and vegetables into different groups using scientific language, e.g. roots, bark, vegetables.

2 CHAROSET

L.O. Identify and describe the basic structure of a variety of common flowering plants.

- Use Activity Resource 2.6 to prepare children for the activity.
- During the beginning of the Jewish holiday of Passover, candles are lit at night and charoset is made and eaten with Matzah, an unleavened bread. Charoset is easy to make with children because it is a cold-cook recipe (Activity Resource 2.7). In this activity, as children cook, focus on the different ingredients, challenge them to describe what they are doing and use the names of the different ingredients and say which part of the plant they are.
- For raisins, show children some grapes and explain that grapes are dried to make raisins. You can buy cinnamon sticks to show it is from bark.
- User PowerPoint Slide 17 to discuss Charoset.

YOU WILL NEED

- PowerPoint Slide 17
- Activity Resources 2.6 and 2.7 – includes details of ingredients

ASSESSMENT

Subject Knowledge

- Em. With support, children can name some ingredients.
- Exp. Children know which ingredients come from plants and can name parts of plants, e.g. root, stem.
- Exc. Children can identify and name the ingredients, know which part of a plant they come from and make comparisons.

3 CHINESE SPRING ROLLS

L.O. Identify and describe the basic structure of a variety of common flowering plants.

- Chinese New Year is a celebration of spring and Chinese people believe this is a time to put the past behind them so they clean their houses, pay off debts and purchase new clothes. They hang paper scrolls with blessings about new life and new beginnings. Families gather for meals and visit friends. Introduce the topic using PowerPoint Slide 18. Spring rolls are a common food during this festival (see instructions in 'Chinese spring rolls' Activity Resource 2.8). A spring roll wrapper can be used.
- Before cooking, let children observe using their senses including taste to find out about the different vegetables. Focus on describing colour, texture, hard, soft, smell, taste and which part of the plant they come from.
- During and after cooking discuss how the ingredients change.

YOU WILL NEED

- PowerPoint Slide 18
- Activity Resource 2.8 – includes details of ingredients

ASSESSMENT

Subject Knowledge

- Em. With support, children can name some vegetables.
- Exp. Children know which parts of the plant the vegetables come from.
- Exc. Children can identify and name the vegetables, know which part of a plant they come from and make comparisons.

4 STUFFED DATES

L.O. Identify and describe the basic structure of a variety of common flowering plants. Identify and classify.

○ Ramadan is a time of sacrifice and reflection in the Muslim calendar when people's thoughts are with the less fortunate. During Ramadan, people eat only before sunrise and after sunset unless they are sick, very old or pregnant. At the end of Ramadan, Muslims all over the world observe a festive three-day celebration known as Eid ul-Fitr, which is the 'Festival of Fast Breaking'. Fresh dates are eaten at the end of Ramadan because they are a soft, easily digestible fruit containing sugars that give people energy after fasting; show children a picture of a date palm tree and introduce the recipe using PowerPoint Slide 19.

○ Use Activity Resource 2.9 to make the 'Stuffed dates'. Prior to making the recipe, give children a date, tell them it is a fruit and ask them to find and take out the seed inside. Let them eat the date, ask them to describe what it is like, e.g., taste and texture. Does it taste sweet? Then prepare the stuffed date recipe.

YOU WILL NEED

○ PowerPoint Slide 19
○ Activity Resource 2.9 – includes details of ingredients
○ Picture of a date palm tree

ASSESSMENT

Subject Knowledge

○ Em. With support, children can name the date and seed.
○ Exp. Children know that the date is a fruit with a seed inside.
○ Exc. Children identify and name the date and compare with other fruits with seeds inside.

Working Scientifically

○ Em. Children match fruits and seeds to pictures and words.
○ Exp. Children use experience to identify and name different fruits and seeds and plant parts.
○ Exc. Children apply subject knowledge to identify and classify fruits and vegetables into different groups using scientific language.

5 A CHRISTINGLE

L.O. Say which part of the body is associated with each sense.

○ Christingle means 'Christ light' and is a symbol of the Christian faith. Christingles are given to children on Christmas Eve. The orange represents the world, the red ribbon the blood of Jesus and the sweets represent fruits of the Earth. Children can use Activity Resource 2.10 to make their own Christingle.

○ Use PowerPoint Slide 20.

○ Ask them which of the five senses are used when making the Christingle.

YOU WILL NEED

○ PowerPoint Slide 20
○ Activity Resource 2.10
  • Candle
  • Orange
  • Red ribbon
  • Assorted sweets (not hard-boiled)
  • Cocktail sticks
  • Cloves

ASSESSMENT

Subject Knowledge

○ Em. With support, children say which sense they are using and point to the correct part of the body.
○ Exp. Children can say which sense they are using and which part of the body.
○ Exc. Independently children talk about using their senses as they work.

 **TOPIC 3 Polar places**

 **About this topic**

Curriculum link: Year 1, Animals, including humans; Everyday materials

SUMMARY:

In this topic, children plan an expedition to the polar regions, learning about properties of different materials, and a range of living things in the polar regions.

UNITS:

3.1: The expedition

3.2: Polar animals

3.3: Food

ACTIVITY RESOURCES:

3.1: Letter from Antarctica

3.2: A polar adventurer's diary

3.3: The polar adventurer

3.4: Is it a carnivore, herbivore or omnivore?

ONLINE RESOURCES:

Teaching slides (Powerpoint)

Interactive activity: Polar places

CPD video: Polar places

Pupil video: Polar places

Word mat: Polar places

Learning objectives

This topic covers the following learning objectives:

o Identify and name a variety of animals including fish, amphibians, reptiles, birds and mammals.

o Identify and name common animals that are carnivores, herbivores and omnivores.

o Describe and compare the structure of a variety of common animals.

o Describe the simple properties of a variety of everyday materials.

o Compare and group together a variety of everyday materials on the basis of their simple properties.

Working scientifically skills

This topic develops the following working scientifically skills:

o Ask simple questions and recognise that they can be answered in different ways.

o Perform simple tests.

o Identify and classify.

o Use their observations and ideas to suggest answers to questions.

CROSS-CURRICULAR LINKS

This topic offers the following cross-curricular opportunities:

English

o Use science-specific language.

o Using punctuation, draft and redraft sentences about what they have done in science activities.

o Make, write and send a postcard from a polar expedition.

Polar stories

o *The Snowman* – Raymond Briggs.

o *Little Polar Bear* – Hans de Beer.

o *Happy Feet* and *March of the Penguins* films.

o Re-telling and changing stories.

Numeracy and mathematics

o Temperature – use comparative language, e.g. warm, cold, hot.

o Buy and weigh food supplies for the expedition.

History

o Famous polar explorers Robert Falcon Scott, Roald Amundsen, Sir Ernest Shackleton, etc.

o Compare a modern expedition with a historic one.

Art

o Make animal masks for role play, e.g. seal, penguin, etc.

o Paint pictures of animals seen on their expedition.

o Paint with shades of white.

Geography

o Where are the polar regions? Look on globe, map and Google Earth.

o What are the similarities and differences between Arctic and Antarctic needs?

o Find out about weather, transport, housing in the polar regions.

o How animals and explorers survive in cold environments.

Design and technology

o Design and make a tent or a milk bottle igloo.

o Design and make a patchwork square for a class blanket using different fabrics.

o Design and make a polar exploration vehicle using construction materials.

Computing / ICT

o Email questions to the Research Station in Antarctica.

o Use digital cameras or video to record their polar expedition.

 HEALTH AND SAFETY

In this topic, some activities require the teacher to use hot water with children.

 SUBJECT KNOWLEDGE

Keeping warm

A good insulator is air and many of the materials used in clothing, particularly coats, trap air in the material as does wearing layers of clothing. Polar explorers need clothing that will keep the body warm (especially their fingers and toes), that is light and comfortable and that allows the wearer to move around easily.

Whilst insulation is a complex topic that children will work on in depth later in the primary years, this set of activities helps to develop some basic language and use early ideas about keeping warm.

Camouflage

Animals use camouflage to hide themselves from predators so they are not eaten, and also to hide from their prey so they cannot be seen by the animal they want to eat. Animals can camouflage

OUTSIDE AREA

o Go on an expedition to explore the school grounds.

o Pack a rucksack. Pull a sledge. Put up a tent. Have a snack.

o Binoculars. Hand lens. Measuring tape. Camera.

o Torch. Plastic bag (for collecting things). Notebook and pencil.

o Read a map to show route of your expedition.

STEAM (SCIENCE TECHNOLOGY ENGINEERING ART AND MATHS) OPPORTUNITIES

o People who go camping, or have been on any kind of expedition.

o Outreach from local university – scientists who have worked in polar regions.

o Someone who skis or snowboards, to show children their ski clothing, etc.

o Make links with British Antarctic Survey scientists to ask questions online.

Visit

o An outdoor clothing store to find out about what is needed for a camping expedition in winter.

themselves using colour, the shape of their body or behaviour. For example, a polar bear is white and therefore camouflaged against the snow.

The BAS

The British Antarctic Survey (www.bas.ac.uk) provides excellent information about living and working in Antarctica. The site explains that generally the food is the same as that eaten at home, but fresh food is limited so most is frozen, dried or tinned. People working there either eat at the Research Station or take food with them on expeditions. They are limited to what they can carry, so most food is dried so that only water is needed to create a meal.

SCIENTIFIC VOCABULARY: POLAR PLACES

It is assumed that most children know, from their EYFS experience, words associated with the weather or hot and cold places such as *freeze*, *frozen*, *penguin* and *polar bear*, although they might not know how to write and spell them. You can download a Word mat of essential vocabulary for this topic from *My Rising Stars*.

Arctic: the Arctic is the area around the northernmost part of the Earth

Antarctic: the Antarctic is the area around the southernmost part of the Earth

carnivore: an animal that eats mostly meat, e.g. spiders, frogs, owls, polar bears, seals, whales and wolves

flexible: a material that bends easily without breaking

habitat: the place where you will normally find an animal or plant living

herbivore: an animal that eats only plants, e.g. butterflies, snails, caribou, cows, deer, elephants, guinea pigs, horses, pandas, reindeer

omnivore: an animal that eats both meat and plants, e.g. wasps, magpies, bears, dolphins, hedgehogs, humans

waterproof: does not let water through

Key words: adventurer / Antarctic / Arctic / carnivore / clothes / cold / explorer / freeze / frozen / herbivore / ice / icebergs / North Pole / omnivore / penguin / polar bear / sea lion / seal / snow / South Pole / warm / waterproof / weather / whale

 PREPARE THE CLASSROOM

Area 1: Polar camp

○ White sheets or white net curtains
○ Tents/Igloo (igloo toy or tent with white sheet over it and blocks painted on)
○ Winter clothes
○ Different fabrics
○ Sleeping bags
○ Haversacks
○ Frying pan
○ Sledge
○ Maps of Arctic or Antarctic
○ Globe
○ Antarctic and Arctic animals (pictures and soft toys)
○ Fire made from logs, flames from tissue paper
○ 'Polar adventurer's diary' sheet (Activity Resource 3.2)
○ 'Hole in the ice' so children can fish, e.g. a bucket painted blue inside, and set under a large piece of white card with a hole in. Put paper fish with paperclips on the inside and use a magnet on a line and pole as a fishing rod or magnetic fishing rods and magnetic fish.

Area 2: Who am I? I am a scientist

○ This area could become the 'Polar Research Station'. Leave a computer with links to the British Antarctic Survey, so that children can view photographs, create files with photographs of animals, icebergs, etc.
○ Interactive activity – search for a drag and drop Internet activity where children place animals in either the Arctic or Antarctic.
○ White laboratory coats (white shirts) for children to wear. You could limit the number of these to regulate the number of children using the area.
○ Children's goggles or protective glasses to wear to help them take on the role of a scientist.
○ Toy animals for sorting into where they live and what they eat (herbivore, omnivore or carnivore).
○ Polar ice sometimes has animals and plants frozen in the ice, so children could make ice with different leaves, flowers or seeds frozen inside. You could leave some for children to identify using photographs or identification cards or to observe what happens when they are left. You could also include dinosaurs frozen in the ice.
○ Photographs and posters of polar explorers, e.g. Roald Amundsen, Sir Ranulph Fiennes, etc.

3.1 The expedition

GET STARTED

Arrange for your class to receive a letter from the fictitious National Polar Adventurers' Society inviting them to become polar adventurers and go on an expedition to the polar regions. You can use Activity Resource 3.1. Children will be more motivated if it is 'real', even if it is only within the school grounds or to a local park or wood.

LET'S THINK LIKE SCIENTISTS

Use these questions to develop research skills and speaking and listening:
o Why do you think people go on expeditions?
o Where would you like to visit on an expedition?
o What special things would you need to take with you?
o Who was Captain Scott of the Antarctic? What did he do?

ACTIVITIES

1 POLAR PLACES

L.O. Identify and classify.

o At the beginning of this topic, use Google Earth to take children on a journey to a polar region, e.g. Antarctica. Introduce the topic using PowerPoint Slides 1–8. Give children access to video clips, posters, books, etc. about the polar regions. Working in pairs, they can use the different sources of information to collect some key facts about either of the polar regions and share these with the rest of the class.

o Ask children to compare the polar regions and talk about what is the same and different. Give children a range of pictures or photographs of different areas on Earth, e.g. polar regions, deserts, tropical rainforests. Ask children to sort them into their own categories and explain their choices.

o Children could use what they have found out to help create a polar region area in their classroom.

YOU WILL NEED

o PowerPoint Slides 1–8
o Access to Google Earth or a similar resource
o Books, websites and other sources of information about polar regions
o Pictures of different areas on Earth

ASSESSMENT

Working Scientifically

o Em. With support, children sort pictures into groups.
o Exp. Children sort pictures into appropriate groups and explain their choices.
o Exc. Children name, describe and compare different regions of the world.

❷ WHAT DO WE NEED? PLANNING A POLAR ADVENTURE

L.O. Describe the simple physical properties of a variety of everyday materials. Identify and classify.

o Using the information about polar regions, children think about what they would need to take with them. Ask them to think about the climate. What clothes do they need, how much they can carry, e.g. warm, do they need, how much they can carry, e.g. warm, waterproof, lightweight? User PowerPoint Slides 9 to 11 to introduce the topic of clothing and explorers. (Challenge children to fit it all in a rucksack.) What food should they take, e.g. why not fresh vegetables? This works particularly well if children can choose from a range of clothing and food, sort the items into useful and not useful, as well as try to pack them all in their rucksack which might require them to rethink their choices.

YOU WILL NEED

o PowerPoint Slides 9–11
o A range of clothing for summer and winter
o Packets of dried food, tinned and fresh food
o Rucksacks
o Tents
o Other camping equipment

Subject Knowledge

o Em. With help, children choose clothing for their trip and name materials.
o Exp. Children identify and classify materials, e.g. coat, scarf, and are able to say why they have been chosen, e.g. coat keeps me warm.
o Exc. Children choose the items according to the materials and their properties, e.g. because they are waterproof.

Working Scientifically

o Em. Children identify clothing and require support to name materials.
o Exp. Children identify materials clothing is made from.
o Exc. Children apply subject knowledge about materials and properties of materials to identify and classify into groups.

❸ HOW WILL WE GET THERE?

L.O. Ask simple questions and recognise that they can be answered in different ways.

o Use PowerPoint Slides 12 and 13 to discuss people who work in and explore the Antarctic.
o This works really well if an adult dresses up as a polar explorer, such as Scott of the Antarctic and, having researched information about the famous explorer (e.g. how he got there, what he took, what he wore, conditions on polar ice), sets the scene and allows children to ask questions. The visitor could show children photographs or artefacts, e.g. waterproofs, ropes, ice pick, food, ski goggles, maps of Antarctica, compass, first aid kit, ice boots, gloves, and discuss what they are used for, e.g.

YOU WILL NEED

o Activity Resource 3.2
o PowerPoint Slides 12 and 13
o Expedition materials including waterproofs, ropes, ice pick, food, ski goggles, maps of Antarctica, compass, first aid kit, ice boots, gloves, sleeping bags, skis, thermal clothing

sleeping bags, skis, thermal clothing and talk about the properties of the materials.

○ Give children the opportunity to handle artefacts and to ask questions.

○ Ask the visitor to focus on travelling to remote places, e.g. by plane, ship, using skis and snowmobiles.

○ Children could use what they know to complete a day in a 'A polar adventurer's diary' (Activity Resource 3.2).

ASSESSMENT

Working Scientifically

○ Em. Children require help to formulate appropriate questions.

○ Exp. Children ask appropriate questions.

○ Exc. Children apply their knowledge to ask questions and suggest how they can answer them.

④ HOME–SCHOOL ACTIVITY

L.O. Ask simple questions and recognises that they can be answered in different ways.

○ The main aim of this activity is to help develop children's ability to ask and answer their own questions. Create a working wall where children place their questions about polar regions; they could use question stem cards to help form their questions: *Which? Why? Where? Who? What? When? What if?* Children take one or more questions home to find answers and share them with the rest of the class. Encourage children to add information to the working wall, including pictures, photographs and key facts.

YOU WILL NEED

○ Question stem cards

ASSESSMENT

○ Em. With support, children ask and answer questions,

○ Exp. Children ask questions and answer them independently.

○ Exc. Children explore areas of interest using in-depth questioning, e.g. polar explorers.

⑤ WHAT TO WEAR?!

L.O. Describe the simple physical properties of a variety of everyday materials.

○ This activity is great for the role-play area where children choose from a selection of clothing to wear when role playing a polar adventurer. Offer a wide selection of suitable and unsuitable clothing.

○ Once children have 'kitted' themselves out they could take a 'selfie' and write a sentence to say what the clothes are made from and why they have chosen them.

YOU WILL NEED

○ Clothing including shorts, T-shirt, sunglasses, sunhat, goggles, different kinds of gloves, scarves, shoes and boots as well as coats, jumpers and trousers

ASSESSMENT

Subject Knowledge

○ Em. Children choose clothes and need support explaining their choice.

○ Exp. Children make appropriate choices and say why they have chosen them.

○ Exc. Children choose clothes according to the properties of the materials, e.g. warm, waterproof, strong.

6 WHICH MATERIAL?

L.O. Describe the simple physical properties of a variety of everyday materials.
Identify and classify.

o It is easier for children if they are able to handle materials, so give children a range of materials and fabrics to explore. Encourage children to touch them, place them against their cheeks or neck and to sort into groups:

- Will keep a polar adventurer warm.
- Will not keep a polar adventurer warm.

o Give children a range of words to choose from to place beside the materials, e.g. *soft, thick, rough, smooth, cold, warm*. Children could use a camera to take a photograph when they have finished. Alternatively, children could make a mini-book and cut a swatch of material to put in their book or use 'The polar adventurer' (Activity Resource 3.3) which has the outline of a polar explorer on which they could place swatches of material.

YOU WILL NEED

o Activity Resource 3.3
o A range of different fabrics and textiles or warm and cool clothes made of different materials

Subject Knowledge

o Em. Children need support to describe the materials and their properties.
o Exp. Children name and describe the properties of materials.
o Exc. Children use scientific language to name and compare the properties of different materials.

Working Scientifically

o Em. Children can sort materials using their senses but require support to identify and name basic materials.
o Exp. Children can identify, name and classify dif-ferent materials into groups using their senses.
o Exc. Children apply knowledge of properties of materials to identify and classify.

7 INVESTIGATE! GLOVES

L.O. Describe the physical properties of a variety of everyday materials.
Perform simple tests.
Use their observations and ideas to suggest answers to questions.

o Provide children with a wide variety of gloves, which they can explore by trying them on, discussing them with their classmates and classifying them, e.g.:

- Flexible: We can move our hands easily.
- Waterproof: Our hands stay dry
- Warm: Our hands stay warm.

o Ask children how they will test which is most flexible, waterproof and warm. They might suggest:

- Flexible: Wearing gloves and trying to write their name, build a tower with blocks, pick up some small pebbles, or the chocolate game – can they unwrap it with gloves on?

YOU WILL NEED

o PowerPoint Slide 14

Subject Knowledge

o Em. Children use their senses to describe the properties of materials, e.g. *rough,* smooth.
o Exp. Children know properties such as stretchy, bendy, waterproof.
o Exc. Children have extensive knowledge of properties and use a wide range of scientific vocabulary, e.g. flexible, rigid.

- Waterproof: Pouring water over the glove, picking something out of a bowl of water without their hands getting wet.
- Warm: Wearing gloves and picking up an ice cube comparing one glove against another.
- Discuss with children: Which gloves were the best and how do they know? What kinds of materials were used? Did they have any special features? This investigation can be extended to look at socks, hats, scarves, trousers and jumpers.

Working Scientifically

- Em. Children require support to carry out simple tests and describe what they did.
- Exp. Children carry out a simple test and use observations to answer questions.
- Exc. Children extend their test or use equipment to measure, e.g. water.

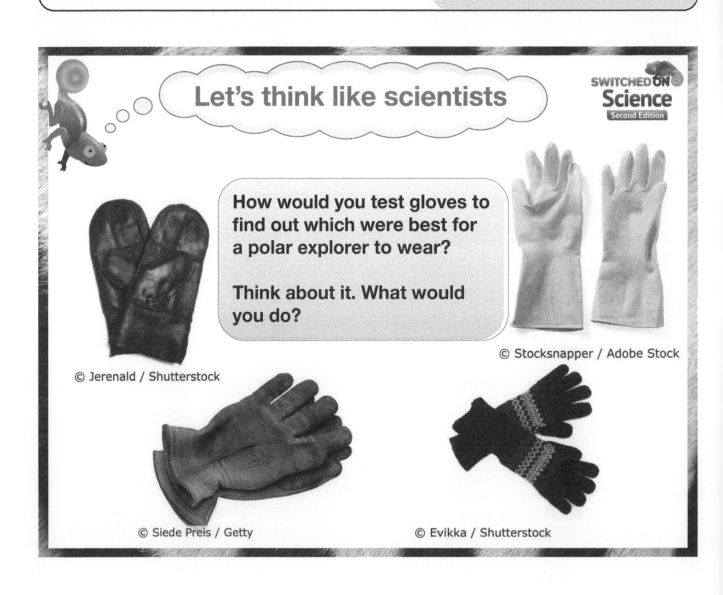

Let's think like scientists

SWITCHED ON
Science
Second Edition

How would you test gloves to find out which were best for a polar explorer to wear?

Think about it. What would you do?

© Jerenald / Shutterstock

© Stocksnapper / Adobe Stock

© Siede Preis / Getty

© Evikka / Shutterstock

3.2 Polar animals

GET STARTED

Activities related to polar animals can take place in different areas, one being the role-play area. Some animals live in the Arctic but not the Antarctic so, during the topic, change the role-play area from the Arctic to the Antarctic to emphasise that different animals live in each.

There are fewer land animals in the Antarctic than the Arctic; however, the Antarctic is rich with sea-life. Help children to understand that human beings cannot live in these areas without wearing special clothes, building special accommodation and taking food with them because it is so cold. All the animals that live in the polar regions have special features to help them survive. Children are not expected to recognise all of these features, but by observing carefully and making simple comparisons they may spot some of them.

LET'S THINK LIKE SCIENTISTS

Use these questions to develop research skills and speaking and listening:

- o How do polar animals keep warm?
- o Which polar animal is the biggest?
- o Which polar animals would you like to see? Why?
- o Why are some polar animals white?

ACTIVITIES

ADOPT AN ANIMAL

L.O. Identify and name a variety of common animals including fish, amphibians, reptiles, birds and mammals. Describe and compare the structure of a variety of common animals (fish, amphibians, reptiles, birds and mammals, including pets).

- o Each group could adopt a polar animal for the duration of the topic. Provide children with a choice so that they develop their understanding of a range of animals that live in these areas, e.g. polar bears, seals, penguins, sea lions, walruses, wolves, reindeer, narwhals, orcas, artic foxes, snowy owls. They could have that animal as a mascot and become experts about their adopted animal, researching information, including:
  - Habitat / what it eats / life cycle / what special features it has so it is able to survive the cold / what its young are like / how it moves / what eats it.
- o Children could record their research by creating their own leaflet, book, video or picture book to show others in the class and visitors, or add their information to their polar adventurer's diary (Activity Resource 3.2).
- o Focus children's attention on finding out the following:
  - The structure of animals, e.g. paws, beak, ears, teeth, fins, claws.
  - Whether the animal is a carnivore, herbivore or omnivore.
  - Whether the animal is a fish, bird or mammal.

YOU WILL NEED

- o Research materials including books and websites
- o Materials for children to present their research, e.g. in a picture book or video

ASSESSMENT

Subject Knowledge

- o Em. Children name some animals and can say if it has fur or feathers.
- o Exp. Children name a range of animals and can talk about obvious differences, e.g. beaks, legs, fins.
- o Exc. Children know which animals live in polar areas and can describe similarities and differences in their structure.

② AM I A HERBIVORE, CARNIVORE OR OMNIVORE?

L.O. Identify and name a variety of common animals that are carnivores, herbivores and omnivores. Identify and classify.

o Introduce the topic using PowerPoint Slides 15–16.

o Most children enjoy learning special scientific words. *Herbivore*, *carnivore* and *omnivore* are words that describe what an animal eats.

o Humans are omnivores and eat both meat and plants. Polar bears are carnivores and eat meat, whilst an Arctic hare is a herbivore and eats plants. Children need to be able to sort animals into these classifications. It will be much easier for children if they have had access to information about different animals through books, selected Internet sites, posters and video clips.

o Provide collections of plastic animals or photographs of animals that children can sort into three baskets labelled 'carnivore', 'herbivore' and 'omnivore'. To scaffold the language, place a picture of an animal that children will be familiar with on each basket, e.g. lion, rabbit and human.

o Use Activity Resource 3.4 and the online interactive activity to reinforce learning.

YOU WILL NEED

o Activity Resource 3.4
o PowerPoint Slides 15-16
o Plastic animals or photographs of animals
o Three baskets
o Labels

ASSESSMENT

Subject Knowledge

o Em. Children sort the animals by their observable features and may say which eat other animals, e.g. polar bear.

o Exp. Children sort animals into carnivore, herbivore and omnivore and can say what each animal eats.

o Exc. Children are familiar with the idea of carnivores, herbivores and omnivores and show more extensive knowledge talking about, for example, polar bears eating seals and seals eating fish.

Working Scientifically

o Em. Children require support to identify and sort animals.

o Exp. Children are able to use given criteria to identify and classify animals.

o Exc. Children apply subject knowledge to identify and classify.

③ THE BIG FREEZE

L.O. Identify and name a variety of common animals that are carnivores, herbivores and omnivores. Identify and classify.

o Ues PowerPoint Slides 17–18 to introduce and discuss this topic.

o Show children video clips that help them to understand why some animals, e.g., polar bears and Artic hares, use camouflage.

o Challenge children to explain what would happen if a polar bear or Arctic hare was red or black. Children might say that other animals would see them and get away, so extend their thinking in terms of consequences, so that children

YOU WILL NEED

o PowerPoint Slide 17–18
o Video clips of various animals
o Art materials

ASSESSMENT

Subject Knowledge

o Em. Children can say what animals eat, e.g. meat or plants.

o Exp. Children can say whether an animal is a carnivore, omnivore or herbivore.

understand that if this happens the animals will be unable to catch the other animals and would starve.

o Create an Arctic or Antarctic frieze and engage children in painting or other art techniques to create pictures of animals and show how they are camouflaged (or not) against the habitat.

o Link with prior learning about herbivores, carnivores and omnivores, asking children to think about the idea that a polar bear is a carnivore, so why does it need to be camouflaged? Ask what a hare is and why it needs to be camouflaged.

o Exc. Children extend their knowledge and decide what other animals in polar regions are.

Working Scientifically

o Em. Children require support to identify and sort animals.

o Exp. Children are able to use given criteria to identify and classify animals.

o Exc. Children apply subject knowledge to identify and classify.

➍ CAMOUFLAGE?

L.O. Perform simple tests.
Gather and record data to help in answering questions.

o Ask children how they could test if the polar animals are camouflaged in their school grounds. What would they do? For instance, children could take paintings or models of polar animals outside and place them against different backgrounds, e.g. grass, soil, trees. They then walk away from the animal whilst counting their steps until they cannot see the animal. Ask children to think about how they could record their results (they could use tables, individual whiteboards or photographs).

o An adult could hide different animals in the school grounds and then time how long it takes children to find each animal and bring it back. At this stage children are not expected to use a stopwatch, but they could record in minutes the time the teacher measured.

o Discuss with the children why some animals can be seen more easily than others, e.g. the white polar bear might stand out against a tree or on the grass, whilst the grey summer coat of an Arctic fox might camouflage it against tarmac or a tree. Link this to the previous activity on camouflage and the problems a polar bear might have if the Arctic was covered in green grass or trees.

YOU WILL NEED

o PowerPoint Slide 19
o Models of animals
o Camouflage paper
o Timing device

ASSESSMENT

Working Scientifically

o Em. Children carry out the test but require support recording results and using them to answer the question.

o Exp. Children carry out the fair test and record results but use experience to answer their question.

o Exc. Children carry out, record data and use it to answer their questions.

⑤ POLAR DOCUMENTARY

L.O. Identify and name a variety of common animals including fish, amphibians, reptiles, birds and mammals.

Identify and name a variety of common animals that are carnivores, herbivores and omnivores. Identify and classify.

- Give children the opportunity to plan and make a mini-documentary video about their favourite polar animal. They could use a soft toy or puppet and explain about where the animal lives, adaptations, camouflage, life cycle, what it eats and whether it is a carnivore, herbivore or omnivore.

- Encourage children to role play being a presenter and use microphones and props. They might create their programme using the role-play area as a backdrop.

YOU WILL NEED

- Camera to record video
- Soft toys of polar animals
- Microphone and other props for video

ASSESSMENT

Subject Knowledge

- Em. Children can name animals and describe where they live and what they eat.
- Exp. Children identify a range of polar animals and talk about carnivores, omnivores and herbivores.
- Exc. Children show depth of knowledge about the polar region, use more extensive scientific language and can link ideas.

Working Scientifically

- Em. Children require support to identify and sort animals.
- Exp. Children are able to use given criteria to identify and classify animals.
- Exc. Children apply subject knowledge to identify and classify.

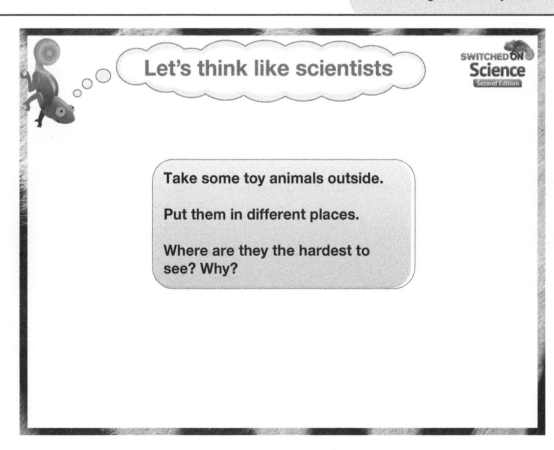

Let's think like scientists

SWITCHED ON
Science
Second Edition

Take some toy animals outside.

Put them in different places.

Where are they the hardest to see? Why?

3.3 Food

GET STARTED

Researchers will take food such as dried soup, dried vegetables, rice, tea, coffee, drinking chocolate, orange drink, biscuits, chocolate, butter, sugar, porridge and dried milk with them.
As part of the role-play area, leave out tins and packages of dried food for children to use to make menus for the expedition. Ask them to think about making the meal interesting and balanced.

LET'S THINK LIKE SCIENTISTS

Use these questions to develop research skills and speaking and listening:
o What kind of food should we eat for energy?
o What kind of food do you think explorers pack on their sledge?
o Why do you think polar explorers need to eat more food than they do when they are at home?

ACTIVITIES

❶ WARM ME UP

L.O. Observing closely using simple equipment.

o Give children the scenario that the polar adventurers have stopped during their expedition to make a warm drink. This is a good small group activity where children work with an adult to make hot chocolate. At each stage, children could take photographs of the process and then use them to write a set of instructions for someone else to use.

o As they make the hot chocolate, ask children to observe closely what happens to the ingredients. Ask them what they think would happen if cold water was used instead of hot, then let them try and compare the results.

YOU WILL NEED
o Mugs
o Hot chocolate powder
o Kettle (for adult use)
o Spoons

ASSESSMENT

Working Scientifically
o Em. Children describe making hot chocolate and, with help, can describe some of the changes that take place.
o Exp. Children talk about the changes they observed.
o Exc. Based on their observations, children suggest other questions, e.g. what if we used milk, less hot chocolate?

❷ SOUP

L.O. Observe closely using simple equipment. Use their observations and ideas to suggest answers to questions.

o A packet soup mix is great for developing observation by challenging children to used hand lenses to observe the mix prior to cooking and then comparing how the soup mix changes when water is added. Before you start, check that no child has an allergy to packet soup.

YOU WILL NEED
o Packet soup mix including vegetables
o Hand lenses or digital microscope
o Plastic containers for separating ingredients

- Give children a sample of the packet mix to sort and classify the different vegetables that are in the soup. Encourage children to use their senses of sight, taste and smell.
- Children use a hand lens or digital microscope to look at the different dried vegetables. Ask them to sort the different dried vegetables into an empty ice cube tray or plastic containers and label them with the name of the vegetable. They could compare the dried vegetables with fresh. Children then pour warm water over them and watch how they reconstitute, then taste them, making comparisons before and after.
- Once they have explored the mix they could, with adult support, make soup for the rest of the class to eat. Discuss with children why polar explorers take dried food on expeditions and not canned or fresh vegetables to make their own soup.

ASSESSMENT

Working Scientifically

- Em. With help, children talk about some of the changes observed.
- Exp. Children talk about the changes they observed when the soup mix was added to water and ask questions related to observations.
- Exc. Based on their observations, children suggest other questions, e.g. What if we left the mix in water for longer? What if we used cold water? Could we dry our own vegetables?

3 PORRIDGE

L.O. Observing closely using simple equipment. Use their observations and ideas to suggest answers to questions.

- Ask children to think about what would happen if they only ate biscuits and chocolate on their expedition to a polar region. Would it be a good thing to do? Would it be good for them?
- People on polar expeditions take food that is good for them. Porridge is a good source of energy. It is rich in fibre and can help to fight infections, so is an excellent food to take on an expedition. It is also dry food and not heavy to carry and can quickly be made into hot food.
- Make porridge with children (remember to check any allergies), so that they can observe changes. Before you begin let children taste the oats so that they can compare them once cooked. Children could also use a hand lens or digital microscope to look at the oats before and after cooking. Which is best: porridge made with normal milk, dried milk or water? What could we add to our porridge, to make it healthier, e.g. dried bananas, raisins, dried apple?

YOU WILL NEED

- Porridge oats
- Milk and / or dried milk
- Digital microscope or hand lens
- Fruit to add to porridge, e.g. bananas, raisins

ASSESSMENT

Working Scientifically

- Em. With help, children talk about some changes and are supported in asking their own questions.
- Exp. Children describe the changes they observed when the porridge was cooked and share their ideas, e.g. why it changed.
- Exc. Based on their observations, children suggest new questions, e.g. What if we used cold water? Could we dry our own fruits?, and how to answer them.

Plants and animals where we live

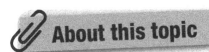

About this topic

Curriculum link: Year 2 Habitats

SUMMARY:

In this topic, children explore their local environment (school grounds or local park) to find out about the plants and animals that live in their locality. Many of the activities could also be carried out in a local botanic garden or arboretum, which has a section on local plants. Children will learn to name and identify common wild and garden plants, including trees, so they are familiar with common names and able to use these in Year 2 and beyond. This topic can also be linked to activities in the Seasonal changes section at the end of this book.

UNITS:

4.1: Our local area

4.2: Birds and animals

ACTIVITY RESOURCES:

4.1: Question wristband

4.2: Tree spotter sheet

4.3: Plant spotter sheet

4.4: Common bird spotter sheet

4.5: Animal cards

ONLINE RESOURCES:

Teaching slides: (Powerpoint): Plants and animals where we live

Interactive activity: Plants and animals where we live

CPD video: Plants and animals where we live

Pupil video: Plants and animals where we live

Word mat: Plants and animals where we live

Editable Planning: Plants and animals where we live

Topic Test: Plants and animals where we live

Learning objectives

This topic covers the following learning objectives:

Plants

○ Identify and name a variety of common wild and garden plants, including deciduous and evergreen trees.

○ Identify and describe the basic structure of a variety of common flowering plants, including trees.

Animals (including humans)

○ Identify and name a variety of common animals including fish, amphibians, reptiles, birds and mammals.

○ Identify and name a variety of common animals that are carnivores, herbivores and omnivores.

○ Describe and compare the structure of a variety of common animals (fish, amphibians, reptiles, birds and mammals, including pets).

Working scientifically skills

This topic develops the following working scientifically skills:

○ Ask simple questions and recognise that they can be answered in different ways.

○ Observe closely, using simple equipment.

○ Perform simple tests.

○ Identify and classify.

○ Use their observations and ideas to suggest answers to questions.

○ Gather and record data to help in answering questions.

CROSS-CURRICULAR LINKS

This topic offers the following cross-curricular opportunities:

Science

○ Identify and name plants and animals in the locality.
○ Compare plants.
○ The needs of living things.
○ Learn what animals eat.

English

○ Learn to write and spell names of plants and animals (nouns).
○ Learn and use descriptive language (adjectives).
○ Use phonics to spell new words.
○ Research using books, posters and video clips.
○ Comparative language.
○ Listen to plant and animal poems.
○ Write sentences.
○ Use labels.

Nature stories

○ *British Trees (Nature Detective)* – Victoria Munson.
○ *British Wild Flowers (Nature Detective)* – Victoria Brooker.
○ *British Birds (Nature Detective)* – Victoria Brooker.
○ *Going on a Tree Hunt: A Tree Identification Book for Young Children* – Jodi Stiriz Bird.
○ *A Little Guide to Trees (Eden Project)* – Charlotte Voake.
○ *RSPB My First Book of Garden Birds* – Mike Unwin.

Numeracy and mathematics

○ Use non-standard measures.
○ Comparative maths language, e.g. longer, shorter.
○ Shape and size.
○ Count leaves, animals.
○ Estimation, e.g. shorter, taller, more, less.
○ Sort into groups.
○ Pictograms.

Computing / ICT

○ Use of Apps for identifying birds, trees, flowers.
○ Use cameras.

Art

○ Flower pressing, using pressed flowers and leaves to create collages, bookmarks.
○ Match colours, e.g. with leaves.
○ Colour shades, e.g. shades of green, yellow in plants.
○ Leaf art, e.g. animals from leaves.
○ Leaf printing.
○ Make collages using natural materials, e.g. twigs, leaves.
○ Twig and leaf impressions / casts or plaques in clay or dough.
○ Clay animals on trees.

Music

○ Make sounds, e.g. mimicking animals, wind in trees.
○ Use natural materials to make musical instruments, e.g. twigs and rice in plastic bottle to make a rain stick.
○ Listen to and sing songs about plants and animals.

Geography

○ Map the location of plants and animals in the school grounds.
○ Compare locality with other habitats, e.g. rainforest, desert.

PE

○ Animal and movements – children creating individual, pair and group dances.
○ Plant movements, e.g. trees swaying, bending, leaves falling, seeds spinning – children creating sequences.

HEALTH AND SAFETY

In this topic, some activities include handling plants and animals; check with children for any allergies and make sure children wash their hands after activities.

SCIENTIFIC VOCABULARY: Plants and animals where we live

It is assumed that most children know, from their EYFS experience, words such as *plant, animal, tree* and *bird*, although they might not know how to write and spell them. You can download a Word mat of essential vocabulary for this topic from *My Rising Stars*.

amphibians: have a soft, moist skin protected by a layer of slime; they live in moist places or near water to keep their bodies from drying out

animal: a living thing that breathes and can move around on its own

birds: have feathers, wings, lay eggs and are warm-blooded

fish: lives and breathes in water

flowers: the part of a plant that blossoms and produces seeds

habitat: a home for plants and animals

identify: to know what something is

mammal: an animal that has a backbone, breathes air, has a backbone and grows hair

plant: a living thing, for example, trees, shrubs, herbs and grasses

reptile: cold-blooded vertebrates with dry skin covered with scales or bony plates and usually lays soft-shelled eggs

stem: the stalk of a plant

tree: trees are tall, woody plants and they have a stem called a trunk

Key words: animals / birds / buds / feed / habitat / identify / leaves / live / nest / plants / sort / tree / twigs

 # PREPARE THE CLASSROOM

Area 1: Outdoor science laboratory

o Table outside or role-play shed
o Hand lenses
o Containers for collecting
o Trays for observing
o Tweezers
o Laminated identification sheets, identification books
o Tent bird hide
o Binoculars

Area 2: I am a zoologist / I am a botanist

o White laboratory coats (white shirts)
o Magnifying glasses
o Collection of animals, e.g. plastic, toy animals, plants
o Identification books, sheets or cards
o Posters and non-fiction books about local animals
o Paper, card and scissors to make books
o Pictures or posters of scientists in the local environment

 # STEAM (SCIENCE TECHNOLOGY ENGINEERING ART AND MATHS) OPPORTUNITIES

Invite into class

o Botanist or zoologist from a local university or STEM ambassador.
o Representative from a wildlife or nature charity, e.g. RSPCA.
o Someone from the local parks department.
o An artist to work with natural materials with the children.

Visit

o Local park.
o Local arboretum or botanical gardens.
o Local animal rescue sanctuary, e.g. birds, hedgehogs.

4.1 Our local area

GET STARTED

Introduce the topic using PowerPoint Slides 1 to 4.
Explain to children that they are going to find out which animals and plants live in or visit the school grounds or local park. Give children the 'Question wristbands' (Activity Resource 4.1) to make and wear. Don't forget to make one for yourself, wear it and model it to ask questions while exploring the outdoors to find plants and animals.

LET'S THINK LIKE SCIENTISTS

Use these questions to develop research skills and speaking and listening:

o What do you think it would be like if there were no plants or animals in the world?

o Which animals would you like to live in the school grounds? Why?

o Why do you think we have to wash our hands after touching plants and animals?

ACTIVITIES

① WHICH PLANTS AND ANIMALS LIVE HERE?

L.O. Identify and name a variety of common wild and garden plants, and deciduous and evergreen trees.
Identify and name a variety of common animals including fish, amphibians, reptiles, birds and mammals.
Observe closely, using simple equipment.
Identify and classify.
Use observations and ideas to suggest answers to questions.

o Use the school grounds or a local park and ask children to look for different plants and animals and see how many they can spot. If appropriate, children could pick a leaf or a flower from each different plant and place it in a collecting bag. Remind children to use their 'Question wristbands' to ask questions, e.g. What is this?, or How did it get here?

o Encourage close observation and show children how to use their hand lenses: hold the hand lens close to the eye and bring the object up to the hand lens until it can be seen clearly.

o Children could also take photographs of themselves exploring and of the plants and animals they find. When children have completed their collection, sort the items either outdoors or back in the classroom using their own or your criteria, e.g. by size, shape, colour, texture, number of petals, flower or no flower.

o Scaffold language, for example, textures and shape, e.g. *rough, smooth, bumpy, velvety, prickly, oval, triangular.*

o Introduce children to the correct names of the plants that they find, since identification naming is a key part of the learning in Year 1.

o Ask if children have seen or found evidence of animals, e.g. bird feathers, snail or slug trails, spiders and webs. Guide children so that they can search for evidence themselves.

o Encourage children to use correct scientific vocabulary by modelling the use of scientific language, e.g. *deciduous and evergreen.*

o Take photographs of children's activities and use sticky notes to record what children say.

YOU WILL NEED

o Collection bags
o Hand lenses
o Activity Resource 4.1
o Camera
o Sticky notes

ASSESSMENT

Subject Knowledge

o Em. Children require support to find and observe different plants.

o Exp. Children identify plants, including trees.

o Exc. Children name some plants, including trees.

Working Scientifically

o Em. Children are supported to identify a narrow range of plants and animals.

o Exp. Children use hand lenses and use observtions to identify plants and animals and answer questions.

o Exc. Children apply knowledge from observations to identify living things and answer their own questions.

2 WHAT'S MY NAME?

L.O. Identify and name a variety of common wild and garden plants, and deciduous and evergreen trees.
Observe closely, using simple equipment.
Identify and classify.

o Tell children that they are going to return to the area that they were exploring in Activity 1 to find out more about the plants and trees there and see how many they can identify and name. Give children Activity Resources 4.2 and 4.3.

o As children work, encourage them to slow down and take time to observe carefully. Take leaves, match them to the ones on the 'Spotter' sheets and help children to learn the names of the trees or flowers. Remind them to use their 'Question wristbands' to help them find the name of the tree or flower, Make learning names an exciting feature of the activity. You could say that the children are botanists – learning about plants. Give points for learning the correct names. At this stage, learning names is important since it lays the foundations for the work carried out in later primary years.

YOU WILL NEED

o Activity Resources 4.1, 4.2 and 4.3
o Hand lenses

ASSESSMENT

Subject Knowledge

o **Em.** Children require support to match, e.g. a leaf with the leaf shown on the 'Spotter' sheets.

o **Exp.** Children are able to match, e.g. leaves with those on the 'Spotter' sheets and learn the names of trees.

o **Exc.** Children independently work out how they can remember, e.g. the features of a leaf linked to the name of the tree it belongs to.

Working Scientifically

o **Em.** With support, children use hand lenses and pictures to identify plants.

o **Exp.** Children use hand lenses and identification sheets to identify plants.

o **Exc.** Children are able to observe and talk about similarities and differences when identifying and classifying.

3 ADOPT A TREE

L.O. Identify and name a variety of common wild and garden plants, and deciduous and evergreen trees.
Identify and describe the basic structure of a variety of common flowering plants, including trees.
Observe changes across the four seasons.
Observe closely, using simple equipment.
Use observations and ideas to suggest answers to questions.

o Tell the children that they are going to choose and adopt a tree and show them a pre-prepared Big Book to record their observations and findings across the year. Children could vote on which tree they would like to adopt and find out about over the school year. Use lolly sticks and glue to show children how to make a simple observation frame, which they will use outdoors to help focus their observations on small areas of the tree.

o Prior to going out, use PowerPoint Slides 5 and 6 to introduce parts of a tree and evergreen and deciduous trees. Visit a tree and give children time to explore the tree and the area underneath it. Encourage children to use their 'Question wristbands '(Activity

YOU WILL NEED

o PowerPoint Slides 5 and 6
o Activity Resources 4.1, 4.2 and 4.3
o Lolly sticks
o Glue
o String
o Paper
o Crayons
o Masking tape
o Camera
o 'Tree Big Book'

Resource 4.1) to ask questions, e.g. How tall is the tree? or What is the tree called?. At some point, you could collect children's questions, scribing them on mini-whiteboards, then support children to work out how they could answer their questions.

o Make sure that children can take photographs of different aspects of the tree for their Big Book, e.g. the shape of the tree, leaves, trunk, roots with children standing next to the tree for comparative observations.

- How tall is the tree? Is it taller or shorter than, for example, a shed or the school roof?

- Is it a deciduous or an evergreen tree?

- How big is the trunk of the tree? Measure using a string and then children's feet, hands.

- Children sketch and take photographs of the tree.

- Take bark rubbings using masking tape to fix their paper on the tree, observing and discussing, e.g. signs of animals.

- Use found materials, e.g. twigs, leaves, etc. to make a tree on the ground of the playground and identify and label the different parts of the tree, e.g. *trunk, branches, twigs, leaves, roots, canopy*.

In the classroom, children place their work, e.g. bark rubbings, sketches, height and photographs with annotated comments in the Big Book. Ask children to find out as much as they can about this kind of tree at home and bring some facts to put into the book.

ASSESSMENT

Subject Knowledge

o Em. Children are supported, e.g. by choice cards to name a tree, parts of a tree.

o Exp. Children name the tree, its parts and know whether it is a deciduous or an evergreen.

o Exc. Children know the name of the tree and its parts and whether it is deciduous or evergreen and can compare it to other trees in the area.

Working Scientifically

o Em. Children require support to make observations about the tree and talk about them.

o Exp. Children are able to make and record a range of observations about the tree.

o Exc. Children use their observations to ask new questions and suggest answers to them.

④ LEAVES

L.O. Identify and name a variety of common wild and garden plants, and deciduous and evergreen trees.
Identify and describe the basic structure of a variety of common flowering plants, including trees.
Ask simple questions and recognise that they can be answered in different ways.
Observe closely, using simple equipment.
Identify and classify.

o Children work in pairs and are challenged to find as many leaves on the ground as they can in one minute. They use their 'Question wristbands' (Activity Resource 4.1) to ask and answer questions about the leaves in their collection.

o Show children PowerPoint Slide 7 and discuss the similarities and differences between leaves and whether their trees are either deciduous or evergreen.

o Children collect a range of leaves from trees (and / or other plants) and use them to ask questions using their 'Question wristband'. They could ask questions and suggest ways of answering their questions, such as:

YOU WILL NEED

o PowerPoint Slide 7

o Activity Resources 4.1 and 4.2

o Tape measures or string

o Hand lenses

o Tree Big Book / large paper

ASSESSMENT

Subject Knowledge

o Em. Children are supported to name the tree the leaf comes from.

o Exp. Children use the 'Tree spotter' sheet to identify the name of the tree that the leaf came from and decide whether it is deciduous or evergreen.

o Exc. Children name the tree the leaf came from without using the Tree spotter sheet.

- *What* is the name of the tree / plant this leaf came from? (Use Activity Resource 4.2, 'Tree spotter' sheet.)
- *Where* was the leaf found? Measure how far from the tree their leaf was found.
- *Which* leaf is the biggest? Note the similarities and differences between leaves.
- *Who* found the most interesting leaf? Comparing similarities and differences with other children.
- *How* did the holes in the leaf get there?
- *Why* do leaves have veins and are they all the same? Classifying leaves according to pattern of veins.
- Other ways of sorting leaves, are, e.g. in order of, size, shape, hairy, spikey, one leaf, made up of more than one leaf (leaflets) colour (light green to dark green).
- Children record their work in the class Big Book from Activity 3, or on a large cut-out of one of their leaves.

Working Scientifically
- Em. Children require support in asking questions about their leaf collection.
- Exp. Children use their 'Question wristbands' to ask questions and use observations to answer them.
- Exc. Children independently ask questions and use observations to answer them.

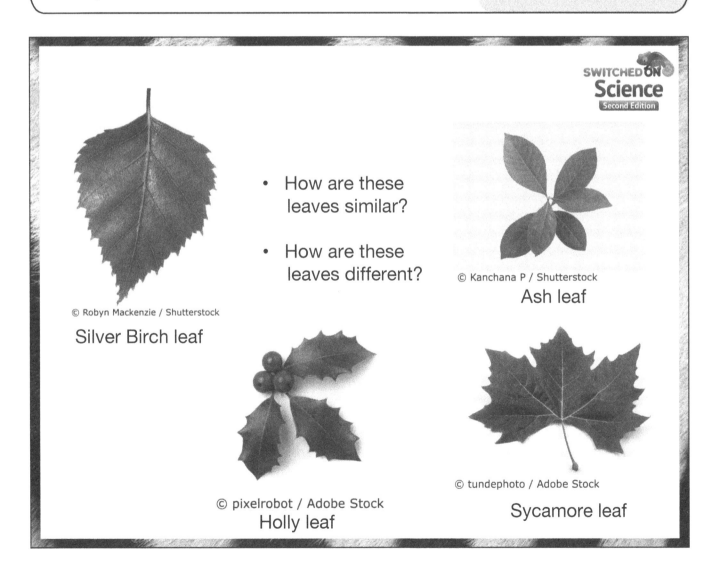

SWITCHED ON
Science
Second Edition

- How are these leaves similar?

- How are these leaves different?

© Robyn Mackenzie / Shutterstock
Silver Birch leaf

© Kanchana P / Shutterstock
Ash leaf

© pixelrobot / Adobe Stock
Holly leaf

© tundephoto / Adobe Stock
Sycamore leaf

4.2 Birds and animals

GET STARTED

Tell children they are going to create a bird hide in the classroom (or school grounds outside the classroom) so they can bird watch to find out which birds visit. Ask children for their ideas; you could show them video clips of bird hides being used. Ask them to list the things that mean an animal is a bird, e.g. beak, feathers, two legs, lays eggs. You can use PowerPoint Slide 8 to help with this exercise.

LET'S THINK LIKE SCIENTISTS

Use these questions to develop research skills and speaking and listening:

○ What would the world be like without birds?
○ How would you find out how many different animals live near you?
○ Why do people feed birds?

ACTIVITIES

BIRDWATCHING

L.O. Identify and name a variety of common animals including fish, amphibiahns, reptiles, birds and mammals. Describe and compare the structure of a variety of common animals (fish, amphibians, reptiles, birds and mammals, including pets).
Observe closely, use simple equipment.
Identifying and classifying.
Gathering and recording data to help in answering questions.

○ Explain to children they will take part in a 'bird watch' and, over the week, they are going to identify count and record each time they see a bird in the school grounds or during a visit to a park (children could use the 'Common bird spotter' sheet, Activity Resource 4.4). Use PowerPoint Slides 8 and 9 to introduce birds and practise identification of similarities and differences.

○ In the classroom, place posters, pictures, etc. of birds most commonly found visiting the area, as well as a large tally chart so children can record each time they see a bird. Teach them how to use binoculars for watching and identifying the birds. Children should count the birds they see each time it is their turn to identify and record.

○ Use PowerPoint Slide 10 to show children how to record their sightings and, when the birdwatch period is over, use PowerPoint Slide 11 to demonstrate how they can create a class graph to record which birds were seen. Work with children to transfer the data from the tally chart to the graph and ask them questions about the data shown.

YOU WILL NEED

○ PowerPoint Slides 8 to 11
○ Activity Resource 4.4
○ Posters, pictures of birds
○ Binoculars
○ Tally chart
○ Hide area

ASSESSMENT

Subject Knowledge

○ Em. Children need help to say what a bird is, e.g. beak, feathers.
○ Exp. Children describe features of birds.
○ Exc. Children describe features of birds and can compare to other animals.

Working Scientifically

○ Em. Children require help to use identification sheets and record birds they see.
○ Exp. Children identify birds and record observations using a tally chart.
○ Exc. Children make their own tally charts to use at home or at play times.

② MAKING BIRD FEEDERS

L.O. Identify and name a variety of common animals including fish, amphibians, reptiles, birds and mammals.
Describe and compare the structure of a variety of common animals (fish, amphibians, reptiles, birds and mammals, including pets).
Identify and classify.
Gather and record data to help in answering questions.

o Challenge children to think about how they could encourage more birds to visit the school grounds; hopefully one of the suggestions they make is to feed the birds. Show children different bird feeders they can make and use PowerPoint Slide 12 to explain they are going to choose one to make.

o This activity is best carried out in small groups with adult supervision. Photographs or short video clips can be used by children to help them create their own set of instructions for making a bird feeder which can be placed on the school website, newsletter, etc.

o Discuss with children where the best place would be for the bird feeders to be placed around the school grounds and then, over a couple of days, carry out a new bird count to find out which birds are using the feeders. Children should use identification sheets (such as, Activity Resource 4.4) and tally charts once again. Discuss with children how the type of bird (e.g. size and shape of beak) means that some birds will find it easier to use the feeders and compare the structure of different birds.

YOU WILL NEED

o PowerPoint Slide 12
o Raisins
o Bird seed (check nut content for allergies)
o Suet or lard at room temperature
o Kitchen roll inserts
o Plastic bottles
o Wooden spoons
o String
o Mixing bowls
o Scissors
o Activity Resource 4.4
o Camera

ASSESSMENT

Subject Knowledge

o Em. Children need help to identify different birds.
o Exp. Children describe features of birds that help them use the bird feeder they have made.
o Exc. Children describe and compare the features of different birds and can suggest ways that they could feed other birds, e.g. different sizes and beaks.

Working Scientifically

o Em. Children require help to use identification sheets and record birds they see.
o Exp. Children identify birds and record observations using a tally chart.
o Exc. Children make their own tally charts to use at home or at play times.

3 WHICH GROUP DOES THE ANIMAL BELONG TO?

L.O. Identify and name a variety of common animals including fish, amphibians, reptiles, birds and mammals.
Identify and name a variety of common animals that are carnivores, herbivores and omnivores.
Identify and classify.

o Use PowerPoint Slides 13, to 18 to show children animals from different groups, and introduce them to different kinds of animals, birds, reptiles, mammals, fish and amphibians. Encourage children to use their personal knowledge and experience to suggest other examples, e.g. their own pets, animals they have seen. If you have them, children could sort toy animals into groups.

o In pairs, children use the 'Animal' cards (Activity Resource 4.5) to sort the animals into groups: birds, reptiles, mammals, fish and amphibians. Tell children that, as they work with their partner, they should say why they are sorting an animal into a particular group.

o Play 'Shout the group' where you show children a picture of an animal and the class shouts out *birds, reptiles, mammals, fish* and *amphibians*. Alternatively, play 'Animal splat' where children use their 'Animal' cards from Activity Resource 4.5 and, when one of the groups is called out, e.g. bird, one person from each group sticks an appropriate card onto a circle on the wall. You could use PowerPoint Slide 17 to challenge children to work out the odd one out.

o You could extend this set of activities to include what each of the animal groups eats and teach children the terms *carnivore*, *herbivore* and *omnivore*.

o Use PowerPoint Slide 19 and have students write a short paragraph about an animal.

YOU WILL NEED

o PowerPoint Slides 13 to 19
o Activity Resource 4.5

ASSESSMENT

Working Scientifically

o Em. Children require support to carry out this activity.

o Exp. Children ask questions, to identify animals and use a tally charts to record findings.

o Exc. Children ask questions, identify animals, and ask and answer their own new questions.

TOPIC 5 — On safari

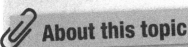

About this topic

Curriculum link: Year 1, Plants, Animals, including humans; Everyday materials

SUMMARY:

Children go on safari to explore invertebrates and other plants and animals in the local area. This topic could be completed in half a term, choosing activities relating to children's experience and interests.
It would be more appropriate carried out in the spring or summer months when there is a greater abundance of invertebrates for children to observe.

UNITS:

5.1: Minibeasts, bugs or invertebrates?

5.2: Comparing ourselves and invertebrates

ACTIVITY RESOURCES:

5.1: Safari observations

5.2: Bug questions

ONLINE RESOURCES:

Teaching slides (Powerpoint): On safari

Interactive activity: On safari

CPD video: On safari

Pupil video: On safari

Word mat: On safari

Editable Planning: On safari

Topic Test: On safari

Learning objectives

This topic covers the following learning objectives:

o Identify and name a variety of common wild and garden plants, including deciduous and evergreen trees.

o Identify and name a variety of common animals including fish, amphibians, reptiles, birds and mammals.

o Identify and name a variety of common animals that are carnivores, herbivores and omnivores.

o Describe and compare the structure of a variety of common animals (fish, amphibians, reptiles, birds and mammals, including pets).

Working scientifically

This topic develops the following working scientifically skills:

o Ask simple questions and recognise that they can be answered in different ways. Observe closely, using simple equipment.

o Perform simple tests.

o Identify and classify.

o Gather and record data to help in answering questions.

CROSS-CURRICULAR LINKS

This topic offers the following cross-curricular opportunities:

English

o Use science-specific language when talking and writing.

o Draft and redraft sentences using punctuation about what they have done in science activities.

o Create a set of rules or instructions for going on safari and for looking after invertebrates.

o Create an estate agent style advertisement for an invertebrate habitat.

o Read and write poems about snails, bees, wasps.

o Children write a story as if they were an invertebrate living in the school grounds.

o Children write descriptions of having been shrunk by their teacher and coming across an invertebrate.

Bug stories

o *Snail Trail* – Ruth Brown.

o *The Ugly Bug Ball* – Michelle Burns and Anissa Freeman.

o *The Very Ordinary Caterpillar* – Garry Fleming.

o *Butterfly Kiss* – Vicki Churchill and Charles Fuge.

Numeracy and mathematics

o Symmetry.

o Counting invertebrates.

o Survey how many invertebrates live in different habitats; use a tally chart.

o Transfer survey data to create pictograms showing the number of different types of invertebrates found in each habitat.

Computing / ICT

o Carry out classification activities.

o Use a camera and video recorder.

o Use Easi-Speak microphones and an Easi-Scope microscope.

o Use Draw or Paint programs to create a new invertebrate. Then use the program to camouflage different invertebrates on a range of colour backgrounds.

Geography

o Using a map of the school grounds, children locate different habitats.

o Children discuss how they can encourage and keep invertebrates in the school grounds.

o Children discuss how their actions can change the school grounds.

o Create maps to show where the invertebrate homes children have made have been placed.

Drama

o Children role play how different invertebrates move, eat, etc.

o Children create plays about hunting for invertebrates or predator / prey.

o Children 'hot seat', taking on the role of an expert, e.g. an entomologist.

Music

o Listen to the song 'There Was an Old Woman who Swallowed a Fly' in pairs or groups and make up their own version.

o Create 'Ugly Bug Ball' music.

o Create music and sounds to represent an invertebrate.

Art

o Look at symmetry in invertebrates.

o Make invertebrates using playdough or papier mâché.

o Paint pictures of invertebrates.

Design and technology

o Design a brand-new invertebrate and its habitat.

o Design and make an invertebrate home (Bug Hotel) for the school grounds.

PE

o 'Ugly Bug Ball' – create a dance for this. Moving like invertebrates.

o Working in groups to make invertebrate shapes and moving collectively.

STEAM (SCIENCE TECHNOLOGY ENGINEERING ART AND MATHS) OPPORTUNITIES

Invite into class

o Use university outreach – invite an entomologist to share knowledge about insects.

o Book 'The Bug Company' to show children and explain about a range of invertebrates.

o Artist to engage children in different approaches, e.g. sponge printing, modelling invertebrates. Create a large sculpture in the school grounds.

o Writer to create poems, descriptions or narrative for a video clip.

Visit

o Different habitats to compare invertebrates living there, e.g. pond, woodland, seashore.

o Pet shop, garden centre, zoo with invertebrates.

HEALTH AND SAFETY

Children should avoid placing their hands in their mouths when handling invertebrates and should wash their hands after handling them. Check with *ASE Be Safe!* for further advice.

In this topic children will be 'Going on a safari' to hunt for invertebrates. The activities in this topic relate to land invertebrates; however, if you have a school pond, many of the activities will also apply to pond invertebrates. Prior to the activity go on your own safari so that you know which invertebrates are in your school grounds or the location you will be working in, and so that you can collect books, videos and photographs of each type to support learning back in the classroom.

SUBJECT KNOWLEDGE: INVERTEBRATES

'Invertebrates' is the correct scientific word; if children can learn 'Diplodocus' and 'Tyrannosaurus Rex', then why not 'invertebrates' – Particularly since it helps them to learn that a vertebrate has a backbone (goldfish, robin, dog, cat, human) and invertebrates do not have a backbone. This is a basic classification that children will need to use as they move through the primary years. Good habits start early. Remember that invertebrates is the collective name for animals without vertebrae and insects are a subset of that group: they have three parts to the body, six legs and usually two pairs of wings.

SCIENTIFIC VOCABULARY: ON SAFARI

It is assumed that most children know, from their EYFS experience, words such as *ant, worm, fly* and *bee*, although they might not know how to write and spell them. You can download a Word mat of essential vocabulary for this topic from *My Rising Stars*.

abdomen: this is the third, last part of an insect and contains the digestive system (stomach), (reproductive organs) and sometimes a sting (e.g. bee and wasp)

antennae: feelers on the head that sense the surroundings and can be used to taste, see, smell and hear

detritivore: an animal that feeds on decaying things such as dead leaves and animals, e.g. woodlice and worms

exoskeleton: an external hard body covering, providing protection and support

food chain: the order that organisms are eaten by each other, most food chains start with a green plant

habitat: a habitat is where an animal lives

head: this is the first part of an insect, which has the eyes, mouthparts and antennae

insect: insects are invertebrate animals that have three main parts to their body: the head, thorax and abdomen, three pairs of legs and a pair of antennae on their head and usually two pairs of wings (although sometimes these are hidden)

invertebrate: invertebrates are animals without backbones

thorax: this is the middle part of an insect's body that has the legs (three pairs) and wings (usually two pairs)

vertebrate: animals that have backbones, e.g. fish, birds, mammals

Key words: abdomen / antennae / detritivore / exoskeleton / eyes / food chain / habitat / head / insect / invertebrate / jointed / key / legs / metamorphosis / pond / sections / thorax / vertebrate

PREPARE THE CLASSROOM

Science laboratory

- White laboratory coats (white shirts) for children to wear. You could limit the number of these to help regulate the number of children using the area.
- Children's goggles or protective glasses to wear to help them take on the role of a scientist.
- Keep invertebrates in this area for study, e.g. giant African land snails, stick insects, butterfly larvae. Keeping live animals in the classroom encourages children to observe, discuss and record changes over time.
- Easi-Scope digital microscope identification keys.
- Collecting pots.
- Big Book to record observations.

Minibeasts, bugs or invertebrates?

GET STARTED

Invertebrates are included because most schools will have these animals in their grounds or areas close to the school, and children are usually intrigued and curious about these animals. Introduce the concept of invertebrates (see Subject Knowledge, page 61) and use PowerPoint Slides 1 to 8 to look at the concept of insects - a subsection of invertebrates.

For this topic, children are invited to go on a safari. The word *safari* comes from the Arabic word meaning 'journey', which is exactly what this is – a journey to hunt for animals. Ask them what they know about safaris. What do people do and what do they take with them? Their ideas will help the class to know what to take on their own safari in the school grounds.

LET'S THINK LIKE SCIENTISTS

Use these questions to develop research skills and speaking and listening:

o How many invertebrates do you think there are on Earth?

o Which do you think is the biggest invertebrate?

o How do you think bees are similar and different to humans?

o How could you find out which invertebrates live in your school grounds?

ACTIVITIES

1 ORGANISING SAFARI RUCKSACKS

L.O. Observe closely, using simple equipment.

o The aim of this activity is for children to decide what they will need to put in their group's rucksack when they go on their safari in the school grounds. Whilst this will take some organising, it is well worth doing as it helps to:

- Organise groups
- Keep equipment together
- Encourage children to work independently and to be responsible for their own equipment.

o Allow children to make their own suggestions for items for their safari rucksack. They might include some of or all of these:

- Camera and / or digital microscope
- Invertebrate identification pictures, invertebrate viewer (bug viewer)
- Notebooks
- Pencils
- 'Safari observations' (Activity Resource 5.1)
- Soft paintbrushes
- White tray, e.g. ice cream container
- Yoghurt pots

o Before children go out, set children the task of creating their own 'Safari rules' either in small groups or as a whole class. These could include the following:

- Be calm and quiet – otherwise the invertebrates will hide away.
- Be very careful – invertebrates are very small and easily harmed.
- Always put the invertebrate back where you found it.
- Take turns to use the equipment and use it carefully.
- Share what you know and can see with each other.

YOU WILL NEED

o Rucksacks

o Paintbrushes

o White trays or containers

o Magnifiers

o Yoghurt pots

o Activity Resource 5.1

o Notebooks and pencils

o Invertebrate pictures / bug viewer

o Camera and / or digital microscope

ASSESSMENT

Working Scientifically

o Em. With support, children can name the equipment in their rucksack.

o Exp. Children can name all the items in their rucksack.

o Exc. Children name and explain what each item is used for.

② WE ARE GOING ON SAFARI!

L.O. Observe closely, using simple equipment.
Identify and classify.

o Naturally, when children first go out they are going to be very excited and flit from one discovery to another. Children do settle down and begin to show each other what they find and talk about it. Don't worry if at this stage they don't identify any invertebrates as there will be lots of opportunities in future activities.

o Tell children that they are going to work in pairs in their groups and that as 'safari explorers' their task is to try to find four different kinds of invertebrates. When they find one, they need to observe it closely using a hand lens.

o The role of the adult working with the children is to listen to their conversations, make comments where appropriate and support children's observations with prompts such as:

• Can you see how big it is?

• Can you see what shape it is?

• What colour or colours is it? If there are coloured pencils in their safari rucksack, they could colour some stripes to show the colour/s.

• How many legs does it have? Does it have 6, 8, 14, more than 14? Or does it have one big foot (e.g. snail)?

• Does it have antennae?

• What are its eyes like?

• How does it move?

o You could give children the 'Safari observations' sheet (Activity Resource 5.1), which helps them to focus their observations. Give them invertebrate guides so that they can try to find out the name of what they find and use PowerPoint Slide 9 to go through the identification procedure with them. The role of the adult is to move around the groups and help them to:

• Slow down.

• Collect carefully.

• Observe the invertebrate and pick out key features, e.g. shape, how it moves, what the habitat is like (where it lives, e.g. under a stone, on a plant).

• Use specific language, e.g. *head*, *thorax*, *abdomen*, *segments*.

o Back in the classroom collate children's first experiences, and pull together what they have found out to help develop the following ideas:

• Where did the invertebrates live (their habitats)?

• Do invertebrates live in the same place, e.g. does a snail live in the same places as an ant or woodlouse? (It helps to have pictures of these for children to recognise.)

• What do they need to live, e.g. food, water, air (oxygen), shelter?

• Which parts of the body did you recognise, e.g. head, thorax?

• Which invertebrates could you identify (name)?

• What do you think the invertebrates eat? Are they *herbivores*, *carnivores*, *omnivores* or *detritivores* (a new word for children)?

YOU WILL NEED

o Safari rucksacks and contents

o Activity Resource 5.1

o Hand lenses

o Invertebrate identification guides

ASSESSMENT

Subject Knowledge

o Em. Children find and observe invertebrates using a hand lens but they require support to identify animals.

o Exp. Children find, observe, identify and name invertebrates.

o Exc. Children identify invertebrates and talk about details using scientific language, e.g. parts of the body, number of legs, its habitat, classifying them into groups, e.g. shell, no shell, more than 6 legs.

Working Scientifically

o Em. Children find and observe invertebrates, say what they look like and how they move.

o Exp. Children find, observe, identify and name invertebrates.

o Exc. Children identify invertebrates and talk about details using scientific language, e.g. *parts of the body*, *number of legs*, *its habitat*.

5.2 Comparing ourselves and invertebrates

GET STARTED

In this activity, children return to the school grounds to look for invertebrates. This time, they look for invertebrates and choose to observe one closely outdoors. It is much better if children observe the invertebrates close to their habitat, using white trays or collecting pots with a magnifying lens.

Discuss with children rules for handling and returning invertebrates to their habitat. This helps to develop children's understanding of the need to respect all living things and their habitats.

LET'S THINK LIKE SCIENTISTS

Use these questions to develop research skills and speaking and listening:
- Are invertebrates living things? How do you know?
- What do invertebrates need to live?
- How are invertebrates different to ourselves?
- What do invertebrates need to live in their habitats?

ACTIVITIES

1 OBSERVING INVERTEBRATES

L.O. Describe and compare the structure of a variety of common animals (fish, amphibians, reptiles, birds and mammals, including pets).
Observe closely, using simple equipment.
Identify and classify.

- Animals including humans use their senses to find out about the world around them (their environment). The table below illustrates some similarities and differences between humans and some invertebrates.

- When children are observing their invertebrates, encourage them to compare what is similar and different between themselves and the invertebrate. For instance, they might look at and compare their own legs and the invertebrate's legs (if it has them).

- Children can work in pairs to do this. Use PowerPoint Slide 9 to introduce the concept of observing an insect closely. Support children with questions to help them focus observations. They might ask:

  • How many legs does my invertebrate have? Are they jointed? Do I have joints? How many? Do the legs have anything on the end?

  • Are there hairs on human legs? Does my invertebrate have hairs on its legs?

  • Where are the legs on the invertebrate's body? Where are mine?

  • How does the invertebrate move? How do I move?

YOU WILL NEED

- PowerPoint Slide 9
- Chalk / mini-whiteboards / paper
- Whiteboard pens
- Magnifiers
- Camera
- Digital microscope

ASSESSMENT

Subject Knowledge

- Em. Children describe animals, but they need support to make comparisons.
- Exp. Children can compare the structure between two animals.
- Exc. Children describe and compare the structure of a range of different animals.

Working Scientifically

- Em. Children describe observations linked to direct questions.
- Exp. Children are able to use observations to identify and classify animals.
- Exc. Children discuss similarities and differences when identifying and classifying animals.

Sense	Humans	Invertebrates
Touch	Our skin is sensitive to touch, we use our hands.	Invertebrates have tiny hairs on their body which sense movement of things and the air around them.
Taste	Our tongue tastes sour, sweet, bitter, salty.	Invertebrates have taste receptors that they use to sense their environment. Butterflies taste through their feet, and honey bees and some wasps can taste using the tips of their antennae. Most invertebrates can taste sweet, sour, bitter, salty.
Smell	Our nose is used to smell things.	Invertebrates use smell to find mates, food, avoid predators and gather in groups using chemical cues. They usually use their antennae, some use their mouths. Many invertebrates use smell to find where food is.
Sight	Our eyes are used to see things.	Some adult insects / invertebrates have either simple or compound eyes. A spider has 2 to 8 compound eyes on its head. Snails have their eyes on the upper tentacle. A dragonfly has compound eyes made up of 30,000 lenses.
Hearing	We hear sounds using our ears.	Invertebrates do not have ears but they detect sound in different ways. For example, grasshoppers detect sound through their abdomen and worms detect vibrations through their skin.
Breathing	We use our noses and lungs.	Most invertebrates have tubes in their outer covering (exoskeleton) that allow them to breathe. Snails have a breathing hole at the edge of their shell.
Eating	We put food into our mouths, and chew using our teeth and push it around using our tongues.	Snails have rows of tiny teeth called radulas that scrape and tear leaves. Butterflies use a long, straw-like proboscis to drink nectar from flowers. Ants have strong jaws and will eat plants and other insects (they are omnivores), whereas worms have no teeth and eat fruit, leaves and decaying animals. They use soil and sand to help them grind the food.

o This activity helps to develop children's close observation skills and encourages them to pay attention to detail. Using phrases such as 'Look again' and 'Look even closer' or 'What else can you see?' is useful to keep challenging children to observe in more detail.

o There are a number of ways that children could record this comparison activity, e.g.:

• drawing their invertebrate on paper or a whiteboard

• drawing their invertebrate using chalk on the playground area.

o If you have a digital microscope, then support children in taking photographs which can later be shown on the interactive whiteboard.

2 ASKING QUESTIONS

L.O. Ask simple questions and recognise that they can be answered in different ways.

o Having spent time closely observing one or more invertebrates, this activity is designed to develop children's ability to ask questions and support them in finding ways to answer them. It is also an opportunity for children to take on the 'mantle of the expert' and to become an authority on a specific invertebrate, so that they can teach other children in their class or around the school about, e.g. snails, worms and woodlice.

o Discuss with children the idea that scientists ask questions about the animals they collect. Use PowerPoint Slides 10 to14 to discuss observations on snails and slugs. Now ask children what they would like

YOU WILL NEED

o PowerPoint Slides 10 to14
o Activity Resources 4.1 and 5.2
o Paper / sticky notes
o Easi-Speak microphone

to know. Give children all or a selection of question stems from 'Bug questions', (Activity Resource 5.2).

○ Tell children that they can only use each question stem card once and they should work in pairs, e.g. children observing a snail might ask:

- What do snails eat?
- How do snails move?
- Where do snails live?
- Are snails born with shells?

○ Children could write down their questions and answers on strips of paper or sticky notes to go in the class Big Book to be used in the next activity.

○ You could also have an adult write questions and answers or children use an Easi-Speak microphone to record them. So that you know which children are confident in asking questions, tell children to put their name against each query.

○ The question stems could also be given to children as wristbands (Activity Resource 4.1) that they can wear outdoors to prompt queries as they work.

③ ANSWERING OUR QUESTIONS

L.O. Ask simple questions and recognise that they can be answered in different ways.

○ Asking and answering their own questions is an important part of working scientifically. Children need to have the ability to do this and they need support in learning how. This activity suggests a way to give a structure to children by using different question stems to help them ask questions, then by sorting those questions into different ways of answering them. Gather children's questions, using the question stems on Activity Resource 5.2, and use the headings below to demonstrate different ways of answering them.

1 **Thinking** – do we already know the answer? E.g. Where do snails live?

2 **Using our senses** – E.g. What colour is the snail?

3 **Using a book or computer** – E.g. What is the biggest snail in the world?

4 **Trying something out** – E.g. Which food does the snail like best?

5 **Researching** – looking in a book or on the Internet. E.g. What kind of snail is this?

○ This is an approach that can be used frequently with other topics so that children develop the ability to ask questions and make decisions on how to answer them.

YOU WILL NEED

○ Activity Resource 5.2
○ Question headings for display

ASSESSMENT

Working Scientifically

○ Em. Children need support in deciding how to answer each of their questions.

○ Exp. Children can make a range of suggestions on how to answer their questions.

○ Exc. Children often challenge suggestions on how to answer questions and can offer alternatives.

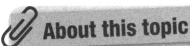

TOPIC 6 Holiday

About this topic

Curriculum link: Year 1, Animals, including humans; Everyday materials

SUMMARY:
In this topic, children will plan what they need to pack for a holiday, and explore the different animals they might encounter at the seaside and the human impact on the environment. You could begin by voting on where in the UK or the world children would like to visit on holiday and work with the most popular place, researching where it is, climate, food, etc. with children deciding what they would need to take.

UNITS:
6.1: Get packed   6.2: By the seaside
6.3: Protect the environment

ACTIVITY RESOURCES: (pages X-X)
6.1: Cold water challenge
6.2: Sunglasses challenge
6.3: Marine biologist challenge
6.4: Seashore animals
6.5: Seashells

ONLINE RESOURCES:
Teaching slides (Powerpoint): Holiday
Interactive activity: Holiday
CPD video: Holiday
Pupil video: Holiday
Word mat: Holiday
Editable Planning: Holiday
Topic Test: Holiday

Learning objectives

This topic covers the following learning objectives:

o Identify and name a variety of common animals including fish, amphibians, reptiles, birds and mammals.

o Identify and name a variety of common animals that are carnivores, herbivores or omnivores.

o Describe and compare the structure of a variety of common animals (fish, amphibians, reptiles, birds and mammals, including pets).

o Distinguish between an object and the material from which it is made.

o Identify and name a variety of everyday materials including wood, plastic, glass, metal, water and rock.

o Describe the simple physical properties of a variety of everyday materials.

o Compare and group together a variety of everyday materials on the basis of their simple physical properties.

Working scientifically skills

This topic develops the following working scientifically skills:

o Ask simple questions and recognise that they can be answered in different ways. Observe closely, using simple equipment.

o Perform simple tests. Identify and classify.

o Use observations and ideas to suggest answers to questions. Gather and record data to help in answering questions.

CROSS-CURRICULAR LINKS

This topic offers the following cross-curricular opportunities:

English

o Read non-fiction books about the seaside and different holiday destinations.

o Writing and sending postcards. Seaside vocabulary.

o Compound words, e.g. seaside, sandcastle.

o Making lists for packing a case for holiday. A list of favourite things we did on holiday.

o Holiday adventure … what happened next?

o Creating captions for holiday photographs.

o Create a travel brochure.

o Using travel brochures.

Holiday stories

o *Tam and Tina Going Camping* – Jack Ireland.

o *Seaside Poems* – Jill Bennett and Nick Sharratt.

Numeracy and mathematics

o Survey favourite holiday destinations – pictograms.
o Survey favourite holiday food, e.g. fish and chips, candy floss, toffee apples, ice cream, ice lollies – graph and handle data.
o Seaside shop – use different coins. Solve money problems.
o Packing – how much will go into a case? Comparing weight – lighter / heavier than.
o Foreign coins – comparisons.
o How many legs? Crabs, lobsters, starfish – calculations.

Art

o Sand pictures and sculptures.
o Collages.
o Marbling – sea patterns.
o Create dioramas.
o Art from countries around the world.
o Wave pictures, mountain-scapes using torn magazine pages to create a landscape.
o Souvenirs from other countries – e.g. bead necklaces, masks, bookmarks, fridge magnets, papier mâché bowls.

Drama

o Role play packing for a holiday.
o Pretend to invent a time machine that can travel any where and any time.

History

o How do we know what holidays were like in the past?
o Where did parents / grandparents go on holiday?
o Compare holiday photographs from the past with the present, e.g. Victorian seaside holidays, souvenirs past and present, postcards.

Music

o 'I Do Like to be Beside the Seaside'.
o Music from different countries, e.g. calypso.
o Instruments from different countries.

Geography

o Use maps to locate holiday destinations. Use maps to locate local airport.
o Look at different coastal features, some natural and others made by humans, e.g. lighthouses.

o Make a glossary of words, e.g. *bay*, *beach*, *caravan*, *sand*, *shingle*.
o Holiday locations – would we like to go there?

Computing / ICT

o Taking photographs for postcards.
o Taking a photograph for a passport.

Design and technology

o Making a photo frame for holiday photographs.
o Making ice cream.

🔷 STEAM (SCIENCE TECHNOLOGY ENGINEERING ART AND MATHS) OPPORTUNITIES

Invite into class

o Marine biologist.
o Geologist to discuss the different rocks found on beaches.
o Photographer to talk about how to take interesting holiday photographs.
o Parent or someone from the local community who is a pilot, train driver, etc.
o Artist to create art using found materials from a beach, sand and pebble art.
o Writer to develop descriptive language, simple poems and stories.

Visit

o A train station or railway museum: look at trains, how do they work, size of wheels, how they have changed.
o An airport: look at systems, e.g. conveyor belts, IT systems, e.g. check-in, safety around the airport, where do planes get their fuel, ear defenders for people taxiing planes.
o Marine centres.
o Beach with a marine biologist.
o Lighthouse.

HEALTH AND SAFETY

Making sunglasses: Children should never look directly at the Sun.

Handling a glass bottle: Glass can be used in science in primary schools, but children should discuss how to use it carefully and to leave the glass for an adult to clear up should it break.

Check with *ASE Be Safe!* for further advice.

 # SCIENTIFIC VOCABULARY: HOLIDAY

It is assumed that most children know, from their EYFS experience, words such as *sea*, *beach* and *sand*, although they might not know how to write and spell them. You can download a Word mat of essential vocabulary for this topic from *My Rising Stars*.

habitat: a habitat is the place where a plant or animal lives

marine biologist: a marine biologist finds out about things that live in the sea

pollution: an example is when humans leave waste in the environment (countryside, seaside, etc.) which harms the habitats and living things in it

sunburn: is when the skin is damaged and goes red because of too much sunlight

Key words: animals / banded wedge shell/ beach / cockle / fish / habitat / limpet / mussel / periwinkle shell / pollution/ protect/ razor clam / recycle / rock pool / rubbish / sand / sea / shell / shell crab /Sun / sunglasses / sunscreen / turtles

PREPARE THE CLASSROOM

Area 1: Marine biologist role play

o White laboratory coats (white shirts) for children to wear.

o Children's goggles or protective glasses to wear to help them take on the role of a scientist.

o Shells for children to sort.

o Pictures of different ocean animals and seabirds.

o Different sand and pebbles to observe using the digital microscope.

o Easi-Scope digital microscope.

o Sea-life collection for classifying.

o Photographs of marine biologists at work.

o Books on the seashore, underwater, oceans, etc.

o Identification keys.

o Big Book to record their observations.

Area 2: Beach indoors or outdoors

o Boats
o Camping equipment
o Empty sunscreen bottles
o Holiday clothes
o Holiday food
o Ice-cream parlour
o Puppet animals
o Rocky pool area
o Sand
o Sea-life collection
o Shells
o 'Slip, slop, slap' slogan
o Stuffed animals
o Sunhats
o Sunglasses
o Swimsuits
o Summer dressing-up clothes

6.1 Get packed!

GET STARTED

If you have the nerve, enter the classroom dressed in your best holiday clothes, sunglasses, wild sunhat or snorkel and flippers; whatever you think will really hook your children, gaining their attention and sparking off interest at the beginning of this topic.

Alternatively, you could walk into the classroom pulling behind you a case on wheels and tell children that you are going somewhere special and they can ask just ten questions to find out where you are going. Then open the case to find out if what you have packed fits with what they have worked out from the questions. Whichever way you capture their attention, explain that you know very little about the seaside and wondered if they knew anything. Then write down their ideas and also questions that they want answered.

You could collect their questions on holiday postcards or place them on beach balls that can be hung from the ceiling or displayed elsewhere in the classroom.

LET'S THINK LIKE SCIENTISTS

Use these questions to develop research skills and speaking and listening:
o What things do you need to pack wherever you go in the world?
o What things would be the same and different if you went to the Arctic one week and then the seaside in a hot country the next week?
o Why do you need to wear sunglasses, suncream and a hat on holiday in a hot country?

ACTIVITIES

PACKING A CASE

L.O. Distinguish between an object and the material from which it is made.
Compare and group together a variety of everyday materials on the basis of their simple physical properties.
Identify and classify.

o Introduce the topic using PowerPoint Slides 1-4.
o Use PowerPoint Slide 5 or, for a lively and humorous starting point for this activity, watch the video 'Mr Bean – Packing for Holiday' – www.youtube.com/watch?v=6r0dr_juOiI. Then give children a suitcase (small like Mr Bean's), just big enough for them to pack for either a beach holiday or a skiing and snowboarding holiday. You might include:

- Boots
- Camera
- Coat
- Flip flops
- Gloves
- Insect repellent
- Jumper
- Lip salve
- Long-sleeve shirt
- Scarf
- Shorts
- Suncream
- Sunhat
- Sunglasses
- T-shirt
- Woolly socks

Do have duplicates of some items, such as lip salve and suncream, which allows for discussion later about the need for them even when holidaying in a cold place.

YOU WILL NEED

o PowerPoint Slides 1-5
o Suitcase
o See activity instructions for list of possible contents

ASSESSMENT

Subject Knowledge

o Em. Children name items but they require support to talk about properties of materials.
o Exp. Children group items linked to properties such as waterproof.
o Exc. Children can explain items are made from a particular material, e.g. flip flops are plastic which is waterproof.

Working Scientifically

o Em. Children identify objects.
o Exp. Children identify objects and classify according to their properties.
o Exc. Children identify objects according to their properties.

o When children have completed this activity, ask them to explain to another group why they have chosen the different items for their hot or cold holiday.

- What are the similarities and differences between the materials and fabrics?
- What are the names of different materials, e.g. plastic, cotton?
- Why have they chosen a T-shirt not a woolly jumper for a holiday in a hot place?
- Why are items such as lip salve, suncream and sunglasses important? Use the interactive activity on *My Rising Stars* to reinforce these ideas.

SUN SAFETY

L.O. Observe closely, using simple equipment.
Performing simple tests.
Use their observations and ideas to suggest answers to questions.

o Children are more sensitive to damage from the Sun than adults. Use PowerPoint Slide 6 as a quick brainstorming activity about what to do to protect yourself in the Sun. Children can suffer from sunburn and heatstroke. Sunburn during childhood can increase the risk of skin cancer and damage to the eyes. Children should be familiar with school procedures to 'slip, slop, slap'; i.e. slip on a shirt, slop on some suncream and slap on a hat, particularly during the summer months. Children should never look at the Sun and they should use sunglasses to protect their eyes.

o Ask children to think about why they 'slip, slop, slap' in the summer at school and when they are on holiday. Collect their ideas. This aim of this activity is to show how the Sun's power cannot be seen, but it can cause changes and damage things. At the beginning of a sunny week, explain to children that they are going to place a big sheet of coloured card (bright colours work best) outside on the tarmac and place different shapes on the card and leave it for the week. What do children think will happen? What will the Sun's rays do to the card?

o Ask them to think again about 'slip, slop, slap'. Why is it important? How can they make sure that they stay safe in the Sun at school and at home? Link this activity to the 'Packing a case' activity and ask children to think about whether they need to 'slip, slop, slap' if going on a skiing holiday and why. Use PowerPoint Slide 5 to discuss the topic.

YOU WILL NEED

o PowerPoint Slide 6
o Collection of sunglasses
o Suncream
o Card

ASSESSMENT

Working Scientifically

o Em. Children carry out a supported comparative test and describe what they did and what happened.

o Exp. Children carry out a simple test, and use observations to say what happened.

o Exc. Children use test results to make links between their observations to draw a simple conclusion.

KEEPING COOL

L.O. Observe closely, using simple equipment.
Perform simple tests.
Use their observations and ideas to suggest answers to questions.

o The aim of this activity is not to teach insulation, but to engage children in a problem-solving activity where they have to make their own decisions and carry out a simple test to answer the problem.

o Create a display of cool bags, fabric bags, plastic bags, plastic containers and plastic bottles of cold water, etc. Beside the display leave out the large 'Cold water challenge' (Activity Resource 6.1) on which a problem is written for children. It asks them to find out which is the best way to keep the plastic bottles of cold water cool on a sunny, hot day at the beach. Children could then use blank seaside postcards to plan their simple test.

o Children could place the bottles with frozen water inside, e.g. a cool bag, plastic container or wrapped in foil, and leave them for part of the day. They might decide to keep everything the same, for the same amount of time and note how much ice melted. The challenge for some children might be to recognise that the water needs to stay frozen, so they need to measure the melted ice (water). If there is a lot of water, the wrapping was not successful.

o Finally, they could reply by writing their own postcard outlining their activity. Draft and redraft their response using a whiteboard before committing their writing to the postcard.

YOU WILL NEED

o Plastic bottles – frozen water
o Cool bag
o Plastic container
o Plastic bag / fabric bag
o Aluminium foil
o Activity Resource 6.1

ASSESSMENT

Working Scientifically

o Em. Children carry out a supported comparative test and describe what they did and what happened.

o Exp. Children carry out a simple test, and use observations to say what happened.

o Exc. Children use test results to make links between their observations and draw a simple conclusion.

 SUNGLASSES

L.O. Describe the simple physical properties of a variety of everyday materials.
Perform simple tests.
Use their observations and ideas to suggest answers to questions.

o Sunglasses are important since they help to filter out the Sun's harmful rays and they reduce the brightness, which makes it easier to see in very sunny conditions. Everyone, including young children, can benefit from wearing sunglasses in bright conditions. Introduce the topic using PowerPoint Slide 7. Leave out a collection of sunglasses for children to look at and try on, so that they can learn how they are made and look at the coloured lenses.

o Ask children to think about the similarities and differences between ordinary glasses and sunglasses.

o What kinds of materials have been used? What properties do those materials have, e.g. rigid, flexible, hard, transparent?

YOU WILL NEED

o PowerPoint Slide 7
o Glasses and sunglasses
o Recyclable materials
o Coloured acetate
o Card
o Activity Resource 6.2

ASSESSMENT

Subject Knowledge

o Em. Children can describe how they made their sunglasses and if things looked lighter or darker with them on.

o Exp. Children name which materials they used for their sunglasses and how they changed what they saw.

o Exc. Children make links to the properties of the material and their use in sunglasses.

○ Give children copies of the 'Sunglasses challenge' (Activity Resource 6.2) and allow them to design and make their own sunglasses, using appropriate materials. Children then test them to see if the lens is too dark, too light, e.g. go outside and see if they make a difference (not by looking at the Sun but at objects). They can take photographs of each other in their sunglasses.

Working Scientifically

○ Em. Children carry out a supported comparative test and describe what they did and what happened.

○ Exp. Children carry out a simple test and use observations to say what happened.

○ Exc. Children use test results to make links between their observations and to ask new questions.

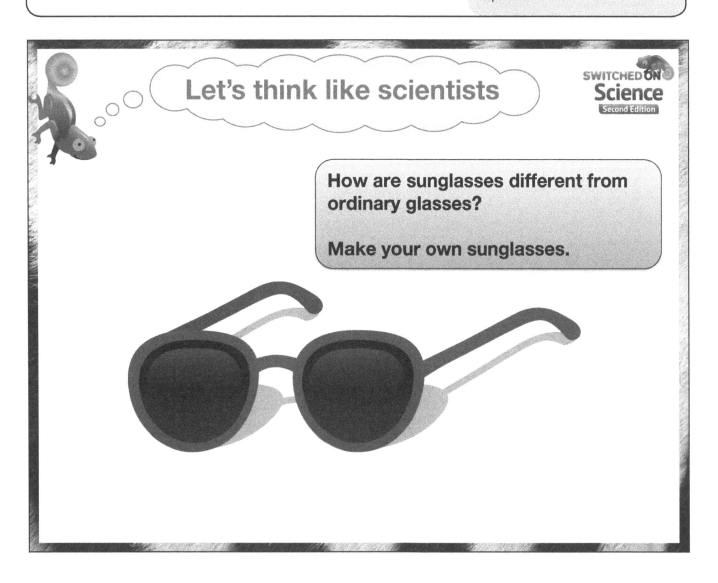

Let's think like scientists

SWITCHED ON
Science
Second Edition

How are sunglasses different from ordinary glasses?

Make your own sunglasses.

6.2 By the seaside

GET STARTED

Set up the sand tray in the classroom or outdoor beach area and hide various sea animals in the sand. Let children know how many animals have been hidden. You could challenge children to find the animals in a set amount of time using a timer. Use PowerPoint Slide 7 to introduce the concept of a marine biologist.

LET'S THINK LIKE SCIENTISTS

Use these questions to develop research skills and speaking and listening:

○ What does the word *marine* mean?
○ Why do you think we need to find out about what lives in the sea?
○ What you think is the biggest animal in the ocean? How do you know?

ACTIVITIES

1 MARINE BIOLOGIST

L.O. Gather and record data to help in answering questions.

○ Give each child in the class the postcard (Activity Resource 6.3), which asks children to find out five things about a marine biologist. This postcard can go home with children as part of a home – school activity with the aim of encouraging children to work independently and also to introduce them to different jobs that scientists do. Children can research using books, asking family or doing safe Internet searches.

YOU WILL NEED

○ PowerPoint Slide 8
○ Activity Resource 6.3

ASSESSMENT

Working Scientifically

○ Em. Children require support understanding the task and how to find the answer.
○ Exp. Children find out the answer to the question.
○ Exc. Children go beyond the question and research additional information and share it with the class.

2 IDENTIFY AND CLASSIFY SEASHORE ANIMALS

L.O. Identify and name a variety of common animals including fish, amphibians, reptiles, birds and mammals.

○ Use PowerPoint Slides 9-18 to introduce the idea of carnivores, herbivores and omnivores and sea animals and life in general.
○ There are many different ways for children to learn about those animals that live in the seas around the UK and on our beaches and rock pools. TV programmes and video clips can help to introduce children to the seashore and, if they have visited the beach, remind them of their experiences. At this level, there are areas of learning to help children to develop, such as to be able to:

  • Identify and name animals such as periwinkles, crabs, lobsters, plaice, black-headed gulls, seals.
  • Say if the animals are carnivores, herbivores or omnivores.

YOU WILL NEED

○ PowerPoint Slides 9-18
○ Plastic animals (marine)
○ Hoops
○ Pictures of animals
○ Activity Resource 6.4

ASSESSMENT

Subject Knowledge

○ With support, children can name animals.
○ Exp. Children use pictures to identify different animals.
○ Exc. Children identify different animals using similarities and differences in their structure.

- Compare the structure of animals, e.g. crab, fish, seagull, seal.
- Classify whether they are invertebrates, fish, birds or mammals.
- Look for key features, such as fish – scales and fins, birds – wings and beaks, mammals – hair and nostrils for breathing.

o Provide children with a collection of plastic animals that live in the sea and on the beach (include birds) for children to become familiar with so that they can learn the names of animals.

o The pictures in Activity Resource 6.4 can be given to children as laminated cards, which they then classify into invertebrates, fish, birds and mammals. The children could sort the cards into hoops or, as a more appropriate context, place the cards in different diorama, e.g. fish in a sea diorama, mammals (such as seals) on rocky islands, and birds on cliffs or a beach habitat diorama. They could also find the animal from a plastic animal collection and place the animal itself in its habitat.

③ MARINE ANIMAL PUPPETS

L.O. Identify and name a variety of common animals including fish, amphibians, reptiles, birds and mammals.
Describe and compare the structure of a variety of common animals (fish, amphibians, reptiles, birds and mammals, including pets).

o Good animal puppets have appropriate colours and features, and provide children with the opportunity to interact with the animal, for example, role playing how it moves, catches prey and hides from predators.

o In small groups, children could use hand puppets to role play how animals would behave in the sea, rock pool or on the beach. In order to do this successfully, children need to build up an understanding of individual animals, and this is where the idea of 'adopt an animal' is very useful. Children choose an animal that they find interesting and research it using books, video clips, posters, etc. to find out as much as they can, thus becoming an expert on the animal. Children should know the animal name, be able to describe what it looks like and key features, e.g. shell, feathers, scales, as well as where it lives, how it moves and what it eats.

o Then children can role play using this knowledge and any experiences they might have gained from visiting the seashore. When children develop the 'mantle of the expert' they could also:

- Participate in 'hot seating' for others to learn from them.
- Make a fact file 'postcard' to share with the class.
- Create a booklet in the shape of the animal for their information.
- Place information on a 'Talk Card' or 'Talk Button' for other children to use.

YOU WILL NEED

o Marine animal puppets
o Books and online research resources

ASSESSMENT

Subject Knowledge
o Em. Children can say which animal they have and talk about its main features, e.g. beak, fur, legs.
o Exp. Children can talk about the animal (or let the animal 'talk' to say what it is, where it lives, etc.).
o Exc. Children carry out extensive research at home and at school and share a wide range of information using scientific vocabulary.

❹ CLASSROOM ROCK POOL

L.O. Identify and name a variety of common animals including fish, amphibians, reptiles, birds and mammals.
Describe and compare the structure of a variety of common animals (fish, amphibians, reptiles, birds and mammals, including pets).

- Use PowerPoint Slide 19 to introduce the topic of rock pools and the creatures that live in them.
- Create a rock pool, preferably outdoors, with shallow water and rocks. Put sand around it (for the seashore) and real or plastic seaweed. You could also stick seashells onto the rocks and place plastic animals in and around the rock pool such as crabs, lobsters, fish, sea anemones.
- Children could visit as 'marine biologists' or as children on holiday to find out what is in the rock pools. They observe and then collect items before using books, posters and audio information around the rock pool to find out information about the animals.

YOU WILL NEED

- PowerPoint Slide 19
- Books, etc. about marine sea-life
- Classroom area as a rock pool
- Puppets, plastic animals, shells, driftwood, etc.

ASSESSMENT

Subject Knowledge
- Em. With support, children can name animals.
- Exp. Children name animals according to their structure.
- Exc. Children make comparisons between the structure of different animals and apply this to identifying them.

❺ SEASHELLS

L.O. Identify and classify.

- Sea shells are the hard, protective outer layer created by an animal that lives in the sea. It was part of an animal's body, but the soft part has probably been eaten by another animal. It is useful here to show children a live snail, to help children understand that this land animal has a shell, and we often find empty snail shells around gardens. Like garden snails, animals that lived in the shells are *invertebrates*, a word that children will have learned in the topic 'On safari'.
- Leave out seashells for children to sort into groups and use.
- Children are fascinated by seashells, but few can name common shells or know anything about the animals that made them. Activity Resource 6.5 has illustrations of common shells found around the coasts of the British Isles. Ask children to identify as many as possible of the ones you bring into the classroom.

YOU WILL NEED

- Collection of seashells
- Activity Resource 6.5

ASSESSMENT

Working Scientifically
- Em. Children can identify similar shells and sort them into groups with help.
- Exp. Children identify different shells and classify them into groups.
- Exc. Children identify similarities and differences and use them to classify shells, and ask questions which they research.

6.3 Protect the environment

GET STARTED

Going on holiday is great, but people are messy and don't always clear up after themselves. This is an important idea, that humans can affect their environment for good and bad. Litter is a huge problem on the beach. Not only does it look bad, it can be dangerous to children playing, it is costly to clear up and it also kills animals. Birds get tangled in it, thinking it is food, and dolphins get caught up in old nets and die. Unfortunately, plastic does not rot down so stays on beaches and in seas, rivers, etc. Use PowerPoint Slides 20-22 to introduce this topic.

LET'S THINK LIKE SCIENTISTS

Use these questions to develop research skills and speaking and listening:
o Where have you seen litter?
o Is litter good or bad?
o Why do you think that?
o What should people do with their litter?
o Why is litter not a good thing at the beach and in the sea?

ACTIVITIES

1 MESSY HUMANS

L.O. Distinguish between an object and the material from which it is made. Identify and name a variety of everyday materials including wood, plastic, glass, metal, water and rock.

o The aim of this activity is to help children to understand just how much stuff humans leave on beaches instead of taking it home with them.

o The list below indicates items that are typically found on a beach which of course, if you are able to visit a beach, you might find with children when you carry out a litter survey. Alternatively, you could create a beach in the corner of the room or outdoors, and put all the items out scattered and half buried in the sand. This should create an interesting starting point for discussion on litter as a human impact on an environment.

- Aluminium foil
- Cans
- Disposable nappies
- Metal bottle tops
- Plastic bottle tops
- Rope
- Sock
- Broken plastic bucket
- Crisp packets
- Flip flop
- Milk cartons
- Plastic bottles
- Plastic cups
- Sweet wrappers
- Broken plastic spade
- Disposable barbeques
- Glass bottles*
- Plastic bags
- Ring pulls
- Shoe

*Glass can be used for this purpose in the classroom. Children should be asked to think about how they should handle this material to make sure that they are safe.

o If collecting from a beach, children should work in small groups with an adult, wear plastic gloves and / or use a litter picker. After the activity children should be given wet wipes to clean their hands.

o Ask the children what they think about the mess, e.g.:
- Why it is there?
- Have they ever seen rubbish on the beach? What did they think?
- Have they heard of the word *pollution*? What do they think it is?
- Which material is the object made from?
- Is the object made from different materials? What are they?

YOU WILL NEED

o A safe collection of litter

ASSESSMENT

Working Scientifically
o Em. Children need support to move from sorting the object to sorting the object according to the material it is made from.

o Exp. Children can identify and sort according to the material objects are made from.

o Exc. Children use properties to identify and classify materials and suggest why those properties might harm animals.

- How do you think the litter could harm animals such as seagulls, seals, etc?
- What should people do with their rubbish?
- Why is litter on the beach a bad thing?
- What problems might the rubbish cause?

○ Children could take it in turns to 'clear up' the rubbish and, as part of this activity, identify the material and classify the litter. Children could put the items in 'rubbish bins' labelled plastic, wood, glass, metal, cloth, then return the rubbish collection to the beach for the next group to classify.

○ By identifying and classifying the litter according to the material, they are also beginning to distinguish between the object and the material it is made from. This is why the rubbish 'bins' are labelled according to the material and not the object. Some objects will be made from more than one material and this can provide useful opportunities for children to discuss and agree upon a final decision.

Which animals would you find in a rock pool?

© Daxiao Productions

September and October

Do these photocopiable activities with your class throughout the year.

HOW WILL WE REMEMBER?

How will you remember what the outdoors was like when you started back to school in September compared to when you went on holiday in July?

- Photographs
- Collect and stick
- Journey Sticks
- Weather records
- Easi-Speak microphones
- Talk Buttons
- Talk Cards
- Monthly calendar
- Diaries

COLLECTING SEASONAL WORDS

- Autumn
- Chilly
- Cooler
- Fruits
- Windy
- Breezy
- Cloudy
- Darker
- Rainy
- Changing
- Cool
- Fog
- Warm

WEATHER

- Use weather symbols to keep a weather chart.
- What kind of week was it?
- How many days were sunny, rainy or windy?
- Create a pictogram and, keep it in a 'Changing Seasons Big Book'.

HOW LONG IS THE DAY?

- Are the days shorter or longer than when you were on holiday?
- Find out what time it gets dark now you are back at school.
- What were you doing in the evening when you were on holiday?
- What are you doing now at night-time?

USE YOUR SENSES

- Out in the school grounds find your favourite:
  - Smell
  - Sound
  - Sight
  - Touch
- How will you record each one?
- Think about photographs, collecting and sticking items, rubbings and recordings.
- Use an egg box to collect things. They are useful because if it is windy you can just close the lid. Collect things that are the same and put them in one of the egg slots. You could collect different textures, e.g. hard, soft, spiky, smooth, silky, crumbly.

COLLECT LEAVES

- How many different ways can you sort your leaves?
  - Different colours
  - Shades of a colour, e.g. red, yellow, orange, brown, green
  - Size
  - Shape
- Put your leaves in order, biggest to smallest and then dark red to orange to yellow.
- What do you think the leaves will be like in November and December?

WHAT ARE WE WEARING?

- What were you wearing when you were still on school holidays?
- What are you wearing now?
- What is different and what is the same about what you are wearing?
- Are the materials you are wearing the same or different as during the school holidays?

WHAT ARE WE EATING?

- How are the foods we eat different and the same as in the summer?
- What plants are ready to eat in our school garden?
- What fruits and vegetables are we eating now, e.g. Victoria plums, blackberries?

WHERE ARE THE ANIMALS?

- Are there animals in your school grounds?
- Look for animals.
- Sketch animals that you see.
- Take a photograph of where you found or saw the animal.
- What food is there for animals to eat, e.g. berries, seeds?
- Back in the classroom, find out more about the animals that you saw.

WHAT CAN WE FIND?

- Use a small lidded container, go outside into the school grounds and fill it with as many things as you can – you have to be able to put the lid on when you have finished.
- Put them in order from biggest to smallest, light colours to darkest colours.
- Sort them into things that were alive and never alive.
- Sort them into different materials.
- Tell a story using the things in your container.

PREDICTING CHANGES

- What do you think it will be like in November and December?
- What will the weather be like? Will it get dark early or late?
- What will the temperature be like – hot, cool, warm, cold, freezing?
- What will we be wearing?
- What will the school grounds be like? What will be different and what will be the same?
- What will the trees be like?
- What animals do you think we will find?

November and December

TALK ABOUT THE CHANGES

- How has the weather changed?
- How have the school grounds changed? What are we wearing that is different? What has stayed the same?
- What are we eating that is different? What kinds of celebrations are we having?
- How have our lives changed because the seasons have changed?
- What do you like about November and December?
- What don't you like about November and December?

COLLECTING SEASONAL WORDS

- Bitter cold
- Freeze
- Frosty
- Ice
- Sunny
- Bright
- Freezing
- Gales
- Snow
- Winter
- Cold
- Frost
- Heavy rain
- Stormy

TWIG HUNT

- Go on a twig hunt; how many different twigs can you find?
  - Short
  - Thick
  - Knobbly
  - Long
  - Smooth
  - Thin
  - Bumpy
- Look at your twigs; can you see a pattern? Which tree does each twig come from? Find out the name of the tree.
- Collect twigs of different shapes and sizes and use them to make a picture or sculpture.
- Look at pictures and sculptures made by other people in your class.
- What do you like about their work?

BARK RUBBINGS

- Get some paper and some crayons and make bark rubbings of different tree trunks.
- How are they the same? How are they different?
- Which pattern do you like best? Why?

WEATHER PICTURES

- Take weather pictures.
- How many different types of weather can you photograph in November and December?
- How is the weather different to summer and autumn?
- What is the temperature like on frosty and snowy days?

WHAT ARE THE TREES LIKE?

- Compare photographs of trees in September and October with pictures of trees in November and December.
- How are they the same? How are they different?
- Look at the shape of a tree silhouette. Paint a tree silhouette picture.
- What has happened to the leaves on some trees?
- Which trees are evergreen and which trees are deciduous?

FEEDING THE BIRDS

- Why is it important that we put extra food out for birds in the winter?
- What kinds of birds come into our school grounds?
- What type of beaks do they have?
- Find out if the shape of the beak tells you what it eats.
- What kind of food will the birds eat? Where will you put food for the birds?
- How do you make a seed fat ball? Make seed fat balls for the birds.

LISTEN TO AND MAKE WINTER MUSIC

- Listen to Vivaldi's 'Four Seasons – Winter'. What winter words does it make you think of?
- How could you make winter sounds? What would you use to make sounds for these words?
  - Shiver
  - Freeze
  - Icicles
  - Slide
  - Slip
  - Howling wind
  - Torrential rain
  - Snow

HOW IS THE WEATHER AFFECTING WHAT WE WEAR AND DO?

- What kinds of materials do we wear in winter? What kinds of materials are waterproof?
- Look at materials under a computer microscope. What do they look like?
- What do waterproof materials look like? What do materials that are not waterproof look like?

DARK NIGHTS

- What time does it get light in the morning? What time does it get dark at night?
- How do people stay safe when out walking or riding a bicycle on dark nights?
- What can you see on a dark night?
- What does the sky look like on dark nights?
- Which patterns can you see in stars at night?
- What is it like when you go out at night?

January and February

COMPARING THE CHANGES

- Look at your pictures and photographs from September to December.
- How are January and February the same as other months?
- How are January and February different from the other months?
- Which season are we in?
- How are our school grounds the same and different?
- How has the temperature changed? Are January and February colder or warmer than September to December?

COLLECTING SEASONAL WORDS

- Blizzard
- Cold
- Gritting
- Melt
- Sledge
- Slip
- Solid
- Change
- Coldest
- Icy
- Perishing
- Sleet
- Snowballs
- Clear
- Freezing point
- Liquid
- Scrape
- Slide
- Snowman

SEARCHING FOR SIGNS OF LIFE

- What is happening in our school grounds? Which bulbs that we planted are beginning to push through?
- Where are they?
- Which plants do we think they are?
- Name the different plant parts.
- What colours are the flowers?
- Photograph the plants.

GROWING POTATOES

Grow your own 'seed' potatoes – these are usually available in garden centres in January and should be purchased then. Choose one of the 'first early' varieties, such as Arran Pilot. (Note that these 'seed' potatoes are actually stem tubers, not seeds or roots.) The stem tubers have buds in and small depressions next to leaf scars (eyes). These are usually concentrated at one end, often known as the 'rose' end. Ask children what part of the plant is a potato.

WEATHER PICTURES

- Take photographs of frost and snow. What are people wearing?
- What are trees like with snow on them?
- What do other plants look like in the snow and ice?
- What is the sky like on frosty and snowy days?

BUILDING SNOWMEN

- How can we stop our snowman from melting? How can we find out?
- Do smaller snowmen last longer than bigger snowmen?
- Does it matter where we build our snowmen – in shade or sun?
- What kind of snow sculptures can we make? Can we have a snow sculpture exhibition?

ICE SPOTS AROUND SCHOOL

- Which parts of the school have the most ice? Where does the ice last all day?
- Where does the ice melt first in the school grounds?
- Why do some places have ice all day and in others the ice melts quickly?
- What is the temperature like in those places?
- Watch the film *Ice Age: The Meltdown.* Some of the animals are extinct. What does that mean?

SLIPPING AND SLIDING

- Why is ice dangerous on the roads and pavements?
- What kinds of shoes are best for walking to school when it is icy? How can we find out and also stay safe?

ICE BLOCKS

- How can we make ice blocks?
- Where will we put them in the school grounds?
- Where in the school grounds do we think they would stay frozen the longest?
- Where do we think they would melt the quickest?
- Why do they melt and stay frozen in different parts of the school grounds? What is the temperature like in those places?

THE SUN

- What is the Sun like during January and February?
- Where does it appear in the sky?
- On what kind of days do we have a lot of sunshine?
- What time does the Sun seem to start to go down, e.g. whilst we are still at school?
- How much sunshine do we get each day? How could we work out how much sunshine there is each day?
- We must never stare straight at the Sun. It can damage our eyes.

HOW IS THE WEATHER AFFECTING WHAT WE WEAR AND DO?

- How do we keep warm?
- What kinds of clothes do we wear? What are the materials like?
- How do animals keep warm?
- Where have some of the animals gone? Which animals hibernate?
- Why do they hibernate?

ANIMALS

- Which animals live in cold places, e.g. the Arctic and Antarctic?
- How do they survive?
- What is special about them?
- What do you know about these animals? What would you like to find out?
- What else can you find out about these animals?

March and April

SPRING WATCH

- What is happening to the trees? What is happening to other plants? What are the birds doing?
- Which invertebrates can you find that you did not see during the winter?
- How has the weather changed?
- What is happening to the length of the days?
- What season are we in now?

MAKE A SPRING WATCH DIARY

- What will you put on the front cover of your diary?
- What will you put in your diary?
- You could take your diary home and find out what is happening in your garden or your local park as you walk to and from school,
- What will you photograph and draw?

COLLECTING SEASONAL WORDS

- Animals
- Babies
- Birds
- Buds
- Day length
- Grow
- Growth
- Invertebrates
- Nest
- Nesting
- Spring
- Temperature
- Twigs
- Warm
- Warmer

SPRING TWIG WATCH

- What are the twigs like?
- What were they like in the winter? How are they different?
- Sketch your twig.
- Look closely to see where the buds are. Can you see a pattern?
- Are the buds opposite each other? Can you spot a spiral pattern?

GROWING TWIGS

- What happens if we cut a twig with buds on from a tree and bring it into the classroom and keep it in a container of water?
- What do we think will happen to the buds on the twigs?
- How can we record the changes?
- Which tree did the twigs come from?

SPRING WEATHER WATCH

- What is happening to the weather in spring?
- How are the temperatures changing? Compare them with the winter temperatures you recorded.
- What are you wearing when you go outside?
- How have the days changed? When does it get dark? Are the days longer or shorter?

JOURNEY STICK

- Make a Spring Journey Stick. Take a photograph of it.
- Compare your Journey Stick with someone else's in your class.
- Hang with string items children find on a walk around the school grounds, or along a line of string. It helps to put something on each end of the stick for safety purposes.

BIRDS' NESTS

- Why do birds make nests?
- Why are they making their nests now? Are all nests the same?
- What do they use to make their nests? Find out how birds make their nests.
- Choose a bird that visits your school grounds.
- Find out what kind of nest it makes.
- Collect materials from your school grounds and use them to make a nest.
- How do you think birds keep all the pieces in the nest together (the glue)?
- What will you use?
- Make a display using your nest and the information you have found out.

MAKE A BIRD NEST BOX

- Invite someone to help you make a bird nest box.
- Which birds visit your school grounds? What kind of nest box do they need? Where in your school grounds could the nest box be placed?
- How will you know if a bird nests in it?
- With your friends, create a set of birdwatching rules that you could use when you visit the bird hide to watch birds.

PLANT PARTS

- How many different plants can you find?
- Find the names the different plants.
- Name the different parts of the plant, e.g. stem, leaves, flower, roots, bulb.

SPRING LISTENING WALK

- Stand or sit still; be very quiet. What can you hear?
- Use the map of the school grounds. Stand in different places and listen; what do you hear? Mark where you heard your sounds on the map and the sounds you heard.
- Do you hear different things in different parts of the school grounds?
- Why do you think we hear different sounds in different places?
- What are you doing in spring that is different to what you were doing in the winter?
- Which other animals are being born in spring?
- Which farm animals are being born?
- Which animals in the countryside are being born? What are their babies called?

May and June

SUMMER IS COMING

- How do we know that summer is on its way?
- How are May and June different to March and April? Look back at your photos.
- What do you think May and June will be like? Will they be warmer or colder, drier or wetter? Will the days get shorter or longer?
- What will you wear in May and June? Will it be the same kinds of clothes that you were wearing in December? Look back at your photos.

COLLECTING SEASONAL WORDS

- Buds
- Colourful
- Flowers
- Insects
- Planting
- Temperature
- Warmer

WHICH PLANTS ARE NEW IN THE SCHOOL GROUNDS?

- Which plants have flowers; are they the same or different to other plants?
- Pick some flowers and press them. Stick them in your Big Book and name the different parts of the plant and find out the name of the plant.
- How many different plants' names can you remember?

PATTERN RUBBINGS

- Take some paper and a crayon outside and see how many different surfaces there are to make a 'surface rubbing'.
- How many different patterns have you collected? Which is your favourite pattern? Why?
- Which patterns were from natural objects and which ones from made objects?
- Which patterns have shapes in them? Make a Pattern Rubbings book.

PLANT A SALAD

- Which salad vegetables do you like? Which salad vegetables do the other people in your class like to eat? Carry out a survey.
- With your classmates, choose your favourite salad vegetables and grow them in some pots outside.
- How will you look after them so that they grow?
- Which parts of the plant do you eat?
- Snails and slugs eat young plants. How will you protect the plants?
- When the salad vegetables are ready, you can all make a salad.

WASHING-UP LIQUID SQUIRTER

- How far can you make the squirter squirt water?
- What kind of force are you using – squeeze, stretch, twist?
- How much will you have to squeeze to make the water jet go 1 m, 2 m, etc?
- How high can the water jet go?
- What can the water jet knock down, e.g. water bottles, empty cans?
- Where did the water go? When you went back out later in the day or the next day, was the water still there?

I SPY...

Play 'I Spy' using different things, e.g. plants, animals, materials, made objects, natural objects.

Switched on Science, Second Edition, Year 1 © Rising Stars UK Ltd 2018

BLOWING BUBBLES

- Why do we play with bubbles more in the summer than in the winter?
- How can you make the biggest bubble and the smallest bubble?
- Which bubble mixture is the best? How can you find out?
- How many different things can you use to make bubbles?
- How can you make a bubble inside a bubble? How do bubbles move in the air?
- What happens when bubbles touch something dry?
- What if bubbles touch something that is very wet?
- What colours can you see in the bubbles? Are bubbles transparent, translucent or opaque?
- Can you make bubbles with just water? What else can you use, e.g. fizzy water?

COLOUR MATCH

- Use crayons or paint matching cards and find out how many different colours you can find outdoors.
- How many different greens, yellows, reds, etc. can you find?
- On one plant how many different colours are there, e.g. on stem, leaves, petals?
- On one tree how many different colours can you see on the bark using a brown colour card?
- How can you record the colours?
- Put the colours in your 'Changing Seasons Big Book' – compare the colours with colours from the autumn.

MAKE A FLOWER

- How can you use things from the school grounds or the garden to make a flower?
- What will you use, e.g. twigs, grass, soil, stones? What will you use for the stem, petals, leaves, etc.? What kind of flower have you made, e.g. daisy, dandelion, sunflower, rose?
- Don't forget to take a photo of your flower.

TINY COLLECTION

- Find a small container no bigger than a matchbox.
- From your garden or the school grounds, fill your container with as many different things as you can.
- What did you collect?
- Sort your collection. How will you sort it, e.g. by colour, size, texture, shape; natural or made, plant or not plant?
- How many things can you name?

WHAT'S IN A FLOWER?

- Ask before you pick your flower (it could be a daisy or a dandelion).
- Find out the name of your flower.
- With a friend take the flower apart very carefully and put the parts on the ground or on a piece of paper.
- How many different parts does the flower have? Which part looks the most interesting? Which part looks the most beautiful?
- Which is the biggest or smallest part?
- Look at the parts from someone else's flower. Which parts are the same, which parts are different?

July and August

LOOKING BACK

- Which season is it now?
- Look back over the year. Use your photographs and other things that you have recorded.
- How has the environment changed since September when you started this class?
- How have you changed?
- What has been the biggest change over the year in the school grounds, your garden or the park?

COLLECTING SEASONAL WORDS

- Dry
- Natural art
- Summer
- Suncream
- Hot
- Rainfall
- Sun
- Temperature
- Measuring
- Shadows
- Sunburn

EATING OUR PLANTS

- What have we grown in our school grounds? What is ready to harvest?
- Can we eat it raw or do we need to cook it?
- What recipes will we use?
- Which part of the plant are we eating? How does it help our bodies?

SHADOW STICK

- Make a Shadow Stick using a plastic flower pot and a stick. Make sure that the stick has something on top so it is not dangerous.
- Explain how the stick's shadow is made. Use chalk and draw over the shadow that the stick makes. Or you could put a small cone at the tip of the shadow. Do this every hour.
- What happens to the shadow during the day?

JOURNEY STICK

- Make a Summer Journey Stick.
- On your Journey Stick put things that you need to stay safe in summer and things that you would like to do during the summer holidays.
- Compare your Journey Stick with the Journey Stick of someone else in your class. How is it the same and how is it different?
- Take a photograph of your Summer Journey Stick.

COLLECT THINGS FROM THE SCHOOL GROUNDS

- Use your collection to make a picture on the ground.
- What will you use to make the frame of your picture?
- What did you use from the school grounds to make your picture?
- Why did you choose those things?
- Take a photograph of your special picture.

SLIP, SLOP, SLAP

- When you go outside, what must you remember to do?

STRING ON THE GRASS TRAIL

- Look at the grass. What colour is it?
- How many different things do you think there are in the grass around where you are standing?
- Get a piece of string that is 1 m long. Put it on the grass and then, using a camera, record the things you see along the string.
- How many different plants are there in the grass?
- What else is in the grass beside plants? What surprised you?

HAVE A PICNIC

- What will you eat?
- What can you use from your school vegetable garden?
- What will you drink? Can you make your own lemonade?
- Who will make what?
- How will you make sure that your food stays fresh and does not get squashed?
- What will you sit on?
- Which games will you play?

SUMMER HOLIDAY DIARY

- Keep a diary of what you do during the summer holidays. Bring it back in September to share with your classmates in Year 2.
- What could you put in your diary, e.g. postcards, photographs, tickets, drawings?

WHERE DOES THE WATER GO ON A SUNNY DAY?

- Make a puddle outside.
- Leave a container of water outside.
- Hang some wet materials or clothes outside. Leave them for a day.
- What do you think happens to the water?
- Use chalk to record how big the puddle was at the start and then at different times during the day. What happened to the puddle?
- Where do you think the water went?

PRESSING PLANTS

- Find a plant and take part of it.
- Press the plant.
- Identify and name the plant.
- Name the different parts of the plant.
- Find out three facts about the plant and write them next to your pressed plant.

PHOTOGRAPH ME

- How have you changed over the year? Which is your favourite season, why?
- What did you learn this year that you have remembered?
- What was the most interesting thing you did in science?
- What have you learned about how the seasons change?
- What do you know about how living things change over the year in your school grounds?

END OF YEAR ASSESSMENT

- Em. Children use the Big Book as support to talk about changes across the four seasons. They can talk about the weather pictures and, with support, say that days are long in the summer and short in the winter.
- Exp. Children talk about changes in the plants and animals in the school grounds or local environment across the year. They know that days get longer and shorter and link certain weather to different seasons.
- Exc. Children link different aspects of seasonal change such as the weather getting warmer with birds nesting, bees appearing, identify plants, e.g. snowdrops, daffodils. They know that day length varies and humans also change what they do during the year.

1.1 How do I feel?

Sad		Happy	
Angry		Surprised	
Excited		Shocked	
Grouchy		Annoyed	
Cheerful		Afraid	
Shy		Worried	

Eye chart

Appointment booking form

Date		Time	
Name			
Class			
Address			

Eye colour	✓ (insert tick please)
Blue	
Brown	
Green	
Grey	
Hazel	

Do you wear glasses ?	
Yes	No

Which letters can you read? ✓ (insert tick please)

a	c	f	g	h	k	m	o	s	t	x	z

Parts of my body cards

Cheek		**Lips**	
Ear		**Nose**	
Ear lobe		**Palm**	
Eyebrows		**Skin**	
Fingernails		**Teeth**	
Hair		**Tongue**	

Switched on Science, Second Edition, Year 1 © Rising Stars UK Ltd 2018

1.5 Taste me cards

You may photocopy this page.

CRUNCHY

FIZZY

SWEET

CHEWY

SOUR

SALTY

HARD

SOFT

BITTER

JUICY

2.1 Hand shadows

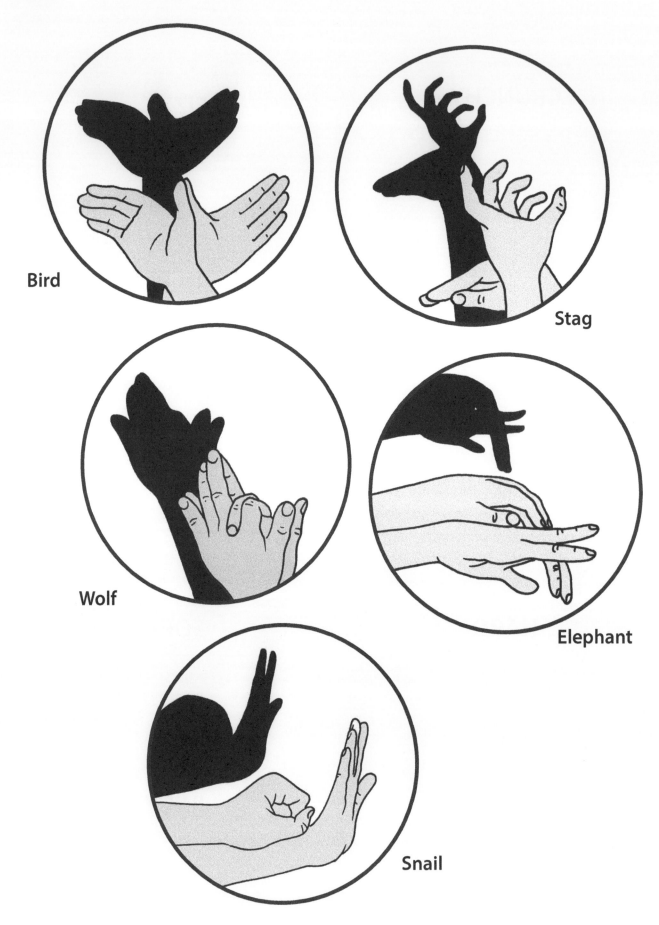

Bird

Stag

Wolf

Elephant

Snail

 2.2 Bottle top clackers

Look at the picture.

Make your own bottle top clackers.

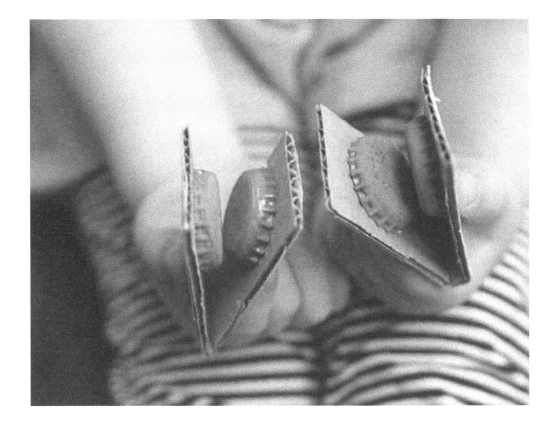

Switched on Science, Second Edition, Year 1 © Rising Stars UK Ltd 2018

Look at the picture.

How do you think the kazoo is made?

Make your own kazoo.

  Switched on Science, Second Edition, Year 1 © Rising Stars UK Ltd 2018

2.4 Ice cube tray xylophone

What sounds can you make with your ice cube tray xylophone?

What songs can you play?

Switched on Science, Second Edition, Year 1 © Rising Stars UK Ltd 2018

Tin can drums

Look at the picture.

Make your own tin can drums.

What will you use to hit the drums?

What different sounds can you make?

2.6 Are you ready to cook?

Have you…

1 washed your hands?

2 rolled up your sleeves?

3 tied back your hair?

4 put on your apron?

5 got out your cooking equipment?

6 got out your ingredients?

Switched on Science, Second Edition, Year 1 © Rising Stars UK Ltd 2018

2.7 Charoset

1 Peel an apple.

2 Grate the apple into a bowl.

3 Squeeze the juice from half a lemon over the apple.

4 Add a handful of raisins.

5 Add apple juice.

6 Add 1 teaspoon of cinnamon.

7 Mix.

8 Eat.

Switched on Science, Second Edition, Year 1 © Rising Stars UK Ltd 2018

2.8 # Chinese spring rolls

You will need:

Carrot Pepper (Bell) Spring onion Beansprouts 4 lettuce leaves Spring roll wrap

Bowl Knife and chopping board Cup Plate

How to cook:

1 Grate the carrot

2 Cut the pepper

3 Cut the spring onion

4 Wash the beansprouts

5 Chop lettuce leaves

How to roll:

1 **2** **3** **4**

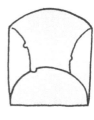

Fold over the left and right sides of the spring roll wrapper.

Keep rolling up the wrap to make a sausage shape.

2.9 Stuffed dates

You will need:

Plate

Teaspoon

Knife

5 dates

10 teaspoons of cream cheese

How to make:

1 Cut dates in half.

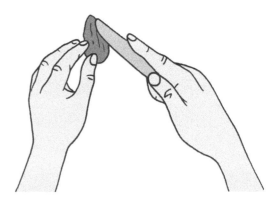

2 Take out stones.

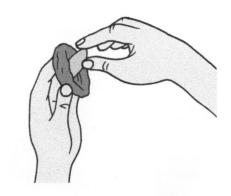

3 Use a spoon to fill dates with cream cheese.

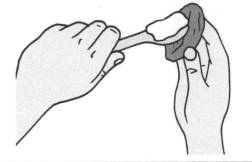

4 Eat and enjoy.

Switched on Science, Second Edition, Year 1 © Rising Stars UK Ltd 2018

 2.10 Christingle

This is a Christingle.
Make your own.
Think about what you will need.
Think about how to work safely.

Letter from Antarctica

National Polar Adventurers' Society
Polar House
Antarctica

Dear Class,

Members of the National Polar Adventurers' Society understand that you are very good scientists. We are looking for a group of scientists to plan and carry out an expedition to two very cold areas on Earth: the Arctic and the Antarctic.

We hope that you will be interested in being involved in finding out everything you can about these very interesting and remote areas on Earth. Please do let us know how your expedition goes and what you find out.

We look forward to hearing from you.

Yours faithfully

Samantha Snowdon
Chair person of the National Polar Adventurers' Society

You may photocopy this page.

Switched on Science, Second Edition, Year 1 © Rising Stars UK Ltd 2018

A polar adventurer's diary

Stick your photo here.

What is the date?

Where am I?

What is the weather like?

What did I do?

What can I see?

The polar adventurer

3.4 Is it a carnivore, herbivore or omnivore?

Arctic fox   **Arctic hare**   **Snowy owl**

Carnivore   Herbivore   Omnivore

Penguin   **Seal**   **Bear**

4.1 # Question wristband

Cut out your wristband and stick the ends together using glue or sticky tape. Make sure that you can get the wristband on and off your wrist.

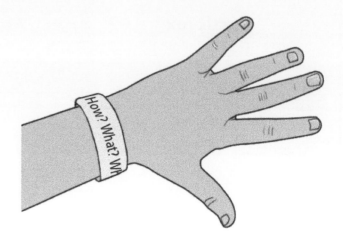

What?
Where?
Which?
Who?
How?
Why?

Switched on Science, Second Edition, Year 1 © Rising Stars UK Ltd 2018

4.2 Tree spotter sheet

Sycamore

Deciduous or evergreen?

Fir

Deciduous or evergreen?

Silver Birch

Deciduous or evergreen?

Hawthorn

Deciduous or evergreen?

Holly

Deciduous or evergreen?

Horse Chestnut

Deciduous or evergreen?

Ash

Deciduous or evergreen?

Oak

Deciduous or evergreen?

Beech

Deciduous or evergreen?

Yew

Deciduous or evergreen?

Switched on Science, Second Edition, Year 1 © Rising Stars UK Ltd 2018

4.3 # Plant spotter sheet

Dandelion		**Scarlet Pimpernel**	
Daisy		**Selfheal**	
White Clover		**Common Chickweed**	
Creeping Buttercup		**Greater Plantain**	
Birds-Foot Trefoil		**Speedwell**	
Yarrow		**Dock**	

4.4 # Common bird spotter sheet

Blackbird		**Magpie**	
Blue Tit		**Pigeon**	
Chaffinch		**Sparrow**	
Crow		**Starling**	
Great Tit		**Wren**	

4.5 Animal cards

Fox ☐

Magpie ☐

Badger ☐

Thrush ☐

Frog ☐

Field Mouse ☐

Toad ☐

Hedgehog ☐

Slow Worm ☐

Deer ☐

Adder ☐

Owl ☐

Safari observations

How many parts have I got?	What colour am I?	How many legs have I got?
1 **2** **3** **Many**		**1 big foot** **6 legs** **8 legs** **14 legs** **Many legs**

Draw your invertebrate.

What shape am I?	What are my antennae like?	Where did you find me?
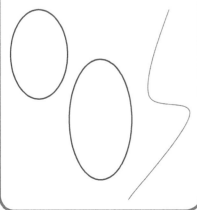		

Switched on Science, Second Edition, Year 1 © Rising Stars UK Ltd 2018

5.2 # Bug questions

What...?		**Where...?**	
How.......		**When...?**	
Why...?		**What if...?**	
Which...?		**Do...?**	
If...?		**Would...?**	
Can...?		**Could...?**	

Switched on Science, Second Edition, Year 1 © Rising Stars UK Ltd 2018

6.1 Cold water challenge

Dear Class,

I am going to the beach for the day. The weather forecaster said 'It is going to be very hot, so make sure that you take plenty of cold water to drink'.

I have got lots of bottles of very cold water but I don't know what to put them in to keep them cold.

Please help me by testing these bags and boxes to find out which is best. You can send me a postcard with the answer to the question, but I will need to know what you did and how you know that the bottles stayed cold.

Thank you for your help.
Dora

Sunglasses challenge

Dear Class,

Sunglasses are really important on sunny days because they help to protect our eyes.

Make yourself a pair of really 'cool' sunglasses using these materials.

Get a friend to photograph you wearing them.

Put your photograph on a postcard, and on the back write about which materials you used and why.

Dora

6.3 Marine biologist challenge

Dear Class

Do you know what a marine biologist is?
Can you find out for me?
Write down 5 things that you have
found out about a marine biologist
on this card.

1 _____

2 _____

3 _____

4 _____

5 _____

Draw a picture of something that has
to do with a marine biologist on the
other side of this card.
Thank you for your help.
Dora

Switched on Science, Second Edition, Year 1 © Rising Stars UK Ltd 2018

Topic 6: Holiday

 6.4 Seashore animals

Common Dolphin	Common Seal	Common Tern
Crabs	Eider Duck	Gannet
Grey Seal	Guillemots	Hermit Crab
Herring Gull	Jellyfish	Killer Whale
Limpets		

Switched on Science, Second Edition, Year 1 © Rising Stars UK Ltd 2018

Seashore animals

Lobsters	Lugworm	Mussels
Plaice	Porpoise	Sand Hoppers
Puffins	Seagulls	Shrimps
Starfish	Terns	Sea Urchin

6.5 Seashells

Limpet shell	Mussel shell
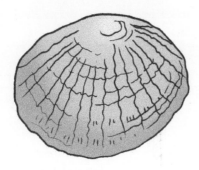	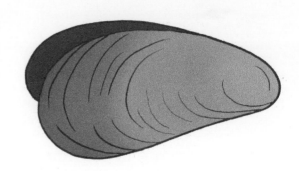
Razor shell	**Periwinkle shell**
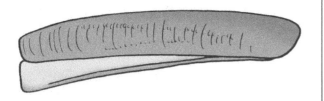	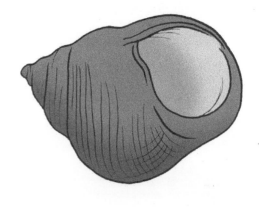
Common cockle shell	**Banded wedge shells**
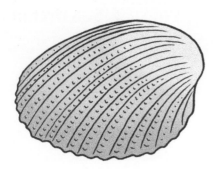	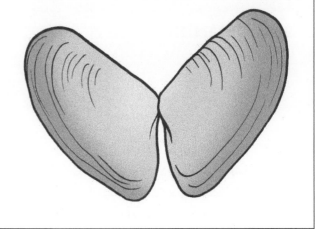

Switched on Science, Second Edition, Year 1 © Rising Stars UK Ltd 2018